STUDIES IN FRENCH LITERATURE No. 32

Advisory Editors
Alison Fairlie
Professor of French and Fellow of Girton College, Cambridge
W. G. Moore
Emeritus Fellow of St John's College, Oxford
Vivienne G. Mylne
Professor of French, University of Kent at Canterbury

RACINE:
ANDROMAQUE

by

PETER FRANCE

Reader in French, University of Sussex

EDWARD ARNOLD

BRESCIA COLLEGE
LIBRARY

43173

© Peter France 1977

First published 1977 by
Edward Arnold (Publishers) Ltd
25 Hill Street, London W1X 8LL

Cloth ISBN: 0 7131 5980 4
Paper ISBN: 0 7131 5981 2

All Rights Reserved. No part of this publication may be
reproduced, stored in a retrieval system, or transmitted in any
form or by any means, electronic, mechanical, photocopying,
recording or otherwise, without the prior permission of
Edward Arnold (Publishers) Ltd.
This book is published in two editions. The paperback
edition is sold subject to the condition that it shall not, by way
of trade or otherwise, be resold, hired out, or otherwise
circulated without the publishers' prior consent in any form of
binding or cover than that in which it is published and without
a similar condition including this condition being imposed on
the subsequent purchaser.

Printed in Great Britain by
The Camelot Press Ltd, Southampton

Contents

Further Reading

The most important thing is probably to read other plays by Racine. The 'Textes Français' edition of the *Théâtre Complet*, edited by G. Truc (4 vols, Les Belles Lettres, Paris, 1929–30) gives original spelling and punctuation, but there are many satisfactory modernized texts; for the present study I have used that in the *Oeuvres complètes*, edited by R. Picard (2 vols, Gallimard, Paris, 1950). No modern text gives the 1668 version of *Andromaque*. A complete sound recording is available in 'L'Encyclopédie Sonore' (320 E.834–5), directed by Georges Hacquard. Important related reading is given in the text, including Homer's *Iliad* and Virgil's *Aeneid*. English readers may find interesting Ambrose Philips's adaptation of *Andromaque*, *The Distrest Mother* (1712).

Among the most interesting modern writings on Racine are R. Barthes, *Sur Racine* (Seuil, Paris, 1962), a wayward and much maligned book, but full of insights; M. Edwards, *La Tragédie racinienne* (La Pensée Universelle, Paris, 1972); L. Goldmann, *Le Dieu caché* (Gallimard, Paris, 1955), translated by P. Thody as *The Hidden God* (Routledge, London, 1964). Works not mentioned later include P. Butler, *Classicisme et baroque dans l'oeuvre de Racine* (Nizet, Paris, 1959); P. France, *Racine's Rhetoric* (Clarendon Press, Oxford, 1965); B. Joseph, *Elizabethan Acting* (Oxford University Press, London, 1951); R. C. Knight, *Racine et la Grèce* (Nizet, Paris, 2nd edition, 1974); J. C. Lapp, *Aspects of Racinian Tragedy* (University of Toronto Press, 1955); O. de Mourgues, *Racine, or the Triumph of Relevance* (Cambridge University Press, London, 1967); R. Picard, *La Carrière de Jean Racine* (Gallimard, Paris, 2nd edition, 1961); E. Vinaver, *Racine et la poésie tragique* (Nizet, Paris, 1951); B. Weinberg, *The Art of Jean Racine* (University of Chicago Press, 1963). A detailed tableau of the literary context is given by A. Adam, *Histoire de la littérature française au XVIIe siècle* (Dormat, Paris, 5 vols, 1949–56) and J. Scherer, *La Dramaturgie classique* (Nizet, Paris, 1950) outlines the dramatic system within which Racine was working. Two useful short introductions to the general history of the period are J. Lough, *An Introduction to Seventeenth-Century France* (Longmans, London, 1954) and P. Goubert, *Louis XIV et 20 millions de Français* (Fayard, Paris, 1966), translated by Anne Carter as *Louis XIV and Twenty Million Frenchmen* (Allen Lane, The Penguin Press, London, 1970). There are innumerable articles and short essays: a good collection, including several specially translated pieces, is *Racine: Modern Judgments*, edited by R. C. Knight (Macmillan, London, 1969).

1. Approaches to Racine

Only about one hundred years after *Andromaque* was first performed, Racine's compatriot and fellow dramatist Beaumarchais protested against the sort of tragic drama it represented:

> Que me font à moi, sujet paisible d'un état monarchique du 18e siècle, les révoltes d'Athènes et de Rome? Quel véritable intérêt puis-je prendre à la mort d'un tyran du Péloponèse? au sacrifice d'une jeune princesse en Aulide? Il n'y a dans tous cela rien à voir pour moi. (*Essai sur le genre dramatique sérieux*, 1770)

Like Beaumarchais, the modern spectator or reader is likely to ask: 'What has it got to do with me?' By the twentieth century Racine's theatre has become for many people, and not just English people, a distinctly alien experience.

Understandably, this feeling of distance can lead to somewhat desperate attempts to bridge the gulf. Producers, critics or teachers may try to ignore obvious features of Racine's plays, such as the high rank of the protagonists or the ceremonial formality of the rhyming verse, in order to bring them nearer to what is supposed to be the taste of our time. So *Andromaque* may be seen as a violent conflict between individuals who just happen to be kings and heroes, but could equally well be the ordinary men and women of the twentieth century. That is not the impression I want to give here—but neither do I want to suggest that *Andromaque* belongs irretrievably to a vanished past.

Above all, however, I wish to avoid the temptation of over-simplification, the temptation of saying too unequivocally that the play means this or that, or that Pyrrhus is this or that sort of person, and of ignoring the many other possibilities offered by the text. There is no unique truth about a play by Racine, or indeed about any poem or play or novel. Different times and different people make what they can of works of the past. Of course there are conventions which make most people at a given time agree that a certain interpretation is fanciful and does not fit the facts. If we are to talk about books at all we shall have to admit that, unlike Humpty Dumpty's words, they do not mean whatever we choose to make them mean—but there is still plenty of room for disagreement.

In this open situation, I could of course use these pages to present as eloquently as possible what would admittedly be *my* version of the play. This is what we have come to expect of the character known as the literary critic; in our century the critic has increasingly become the interpreter or reinterpreter of old texts. It seems to me, however, that it is more helpful to open out the text, suggesting various approaches rather than trying to impose one view. I use the words 'open out' because, as I have just said, there is indeed a problem of access. Racine's plays, particularly when printed, face the reader disconcertingly with their compact phalanxes of regular verse, their long speeches and their lack of stage directions (no 'Exit pursued by a bear' in Racine, alas!). It therefore seems important to suggest something of the diverse possibilities which are there for producers, actors, spectators and readers.

There are perhaps three principal ways of approaching *Andromaque* —as a 'score' for theatrical production, as a text for solitary reading and rereading, or as the work of a particular individual (Racine) in a particular society (the France of 1667). These provide the three chapters that follow. Different people will prefer different approaches or indeed the same person may prefer different approaches on different occasions. None of the three takes precedence over the others. For instance, there may well be a conflict between what we make of a play in modern productions and readings and what we suppose it meant for its first spectators. It would in my view be wrong-headed to use historical evidence as a weapon to beat down modern interpretations; Racine's texts are there for us now, and we cannot change ourselves into seventeenth-century French people in order to read or perform them. Nevertheless, it is undoubtedly true that a historical understanding of the play adds a great deal to our experience of it as something *different*.

Similarly it is sometimes argued that the stage production is what really matters. *Andromaque* is after all a play and was written to be performed, so what we get out of solitary reading is beside the point. But this is to fly in the face of the facts; Racine is read nowadays more than he is performed. The memory of performances we have seen may affect our reading, but careful reading by producers and actors also precedes performance, and the memory of personal reading will leave its mark on the way a spectator watches a production of a play. In fact my division into three parts, like all such arrangements, is only to be justified in terms of clarity and convenience; the theatrical, the textual and the historical are constantly interwoven in one's experience of such a play as *Andromaque*.

2. A Score for Performance

When people talk about *Andromaque*, particularly in schools and universities, they often refer to it as a 'book', and indeed it is as printed texts that many people first meet Racine's plays. Nevertheless, these plays have been continued to be performed over the last three hundred years, and *Andromaque* more often than most. So even if one is restricted to the printed word it is worth while attempting to imagine how a theatrical production can give life and body to what is from one angle comparable to a musical score.

Dramatic Rhythm

In considering *Andromaque* as a play, we need to think of it as an experience that unfolds in time. As such it has, or can be given, a definite rhythm, with a beginning, ending, stopping places, moments of acceleration and so on. It shares the basic features of this rhythm with all French tragedies of the classical period. In these plays the action begins at a point of climax, so there will usually be a slowish exposition scene in which characters explain to one another—and to the audience—what has been happening before the real action begins. Then a 'noeud' or dramatic problem will be created, the tension will mount through a series of confrontations between a small number of characters and will finally be resolved, often by a violent turn of events off-stage, in the 'dénouement' of the last act. One also expects that a series of continuous scenes will build up excitement within each act, and that the playwright will maintain interest by varying the pace from scene to scene. And finally one can be fairly sure that he will follow the rules laid down by theoreticians and confine himself to one main story (unity of action), one scene (unity of place) and the events of one crowded day (unity of time); these 'rules' may have rested on a forced interpretation of Aristotle's *Poetics*, but they helped dramatists to achieve powerful effects of concentration.

Andromaque conforms very well to this 'identikit' pattern of classical tragedy. In his choice of a beginning and end, and in his concentration on one eventful day when a long sequence of events comes to a head, Racine gives his play the thrusting intensity favoured by classical dramaturgy. As for the unity of action, it might at first seem that several things are happening at once: Oreste, having come to Epirus on a Greek mission to claim the surrender of Hector's son Astyanax, is attempting to use this as a way of obtaining his beloved Hermione; meanwhile Pyrrhus, King of Epirus and betrothed to Hermione, is pressing Astyanax's mother Andromaque to marry him and tries to use Oreste's demands as a blackmail weapon. What Racine does, of course, is to twist these different intrigues into one knot, so that any movement by one of the principal characters has repercussions on all the rest. The formula, 'A loves B, who loves C, who loves D, who loves E, who is dead', has often been used to describe the infernal machine of *Andromaque*, and it shows that in the end the action depends on Andromaque. The first three acts gradually push her into the decision to marry Pyrrhus; this decision, taken between Acts III and IV, is probably the main turning point in the play. Given this decision, the words and actions of the characters lead inexorably to the final series of catastrophes.

Nevertheless, even if the play does have this one principal turning point, it is made up of twists and turns, each act bringing a new situation and one or more climactic scenes of confrontation between two of the main characters. These 'battle' scenes are generally preceded by monologues or scenes with confidants in which the main characters express themselves more freely and openly. Within each act, moreover, there is an alternation between long speeches ('tirades') and more rapid passages of dialogue. There may be an overall feeling of inevitable disaster (in retrospect at least), but in detail the play is made up of surprises, contrasts and changes of tempo.

Let us look at Act III as the clearest case of the variety of pitch and tempo with which Racine can hold the excited interest of the spectator. Unlike Act I, this act opens at full emotional pitch, as Pylade attempts to dissuade the furious Oreste from taking violent action. The open emotions of the first scene give way to the calm of Scene ii, where Oreste and Hermione speak formally to each other, hiding as best they can their true feelings. When Oreste has gone, Hermione in her turn can express her feelings more energetically to Cléone, only to have to suppress them and speak formally but mockingly in answer to Andromaque's eloquent speech in Scene iv. A brief exchange between Andromaque and her confidant is followed by a curious piece of oblique sparring in short speeches between Andromaque and Pyrrhus; the speeches grow longer as the two characters employ the full weight of persuasion against one another. Finally Andromaque, left with Céphise, evokes her dilemma in two moving speeches leading to a tense ending where the speeches grow shorter. The audience is left poised in the uncertainty which characterizes the ends of acts.

The act has taken us over the complete range of *dramatis personae*, and the number of actors present on stage has oscillated as follows: 2, 3, 2, 4, 2, 4, 3, 2. Further, the overall rhythm of the act is matched by variations within each scene; characteristically the dialogue will swell out of the rapid and broken exchanges into long, eloquent tirades and then retract again as the protagonists take stock of the situation and prepare to meet a new challenge. To find an analogy for this dramatic rhythm we might think of the growth and breaking of waves and their ebb and flow within a rising tide.

The final act has a movement all its own; here a good deal of the effect is created by the fact that the action is taking place or has already taken place off the stage and is only progressively (and often misleadingly) revealed to the people on stage and to the audience. It is no longer so much a question of confrontation as of the mounting pressure of catastrophic news. The last scene, moreover, brings in some new actors, the Greek soldiers, whose silence should not lead us to underestimate their dramatic importance. *Andromaque* ends in an unusually violent way: Oreste actually loses his reason on the stage (there is no question here of the tragedy that closes 'with calm of mind, all passion spent'), the crescendo movement continues to the end, and even Pylade's last four lines hurry the remaining actors off the stage.

So far I have described some features of the rhythm of *Andromaque* as if they were simply given to the producer. But even here, though Racine's play is a fine dramatic machine, a 'pièce bien faite' in the traditional sense of the expression, there can still be considerable differences of interpretation. For instance, I have spoken of two sorts of movement, that which is internal to particular acts and that which can be perceived in the play as a whole. Both can coexist, but their respective importance will be altered by the way the play is divided up in performance. In Racine's day the acts were separated by proper 'entr'actes', during which candles were snuffed and there might be some sort of musical entertainment; this must have meant that each act was made more of a separate entity, rather as when a novel is turned into a weekly television serial with each instalment ending on a note of uncertainty. Today we should find it odd to have four intervals in a relatively short play, and it is normal for the play to be performed with only one real break. (Occasionally indeed a Racine play is performed without any interval so as to maintain the emotional pressure on the audience, but this is as likely to lead to weariness as to concentration.) If there is to be one interval, the turning point between Acts III and IV seems the obvious place; this is the one occasion when any real break is called for, while Andromaque goes to the tomb of Hector. In all other cases the acts follow one another almost as directly as the scenes within the acts, although one should not forget that several important meetings take place off stage—in particular the second conversation of Pyrrhus and Andromaque, reported in Act II, Scene v.

Apart from this apparently rather trivial but theatrically important question of intervals, the producer has to choose how much to make of the possibilities of excitement and variety which the text seems to offer. Probably no one will want to produce the play at a completely unvarying tempo, but the degree of emphasis given to the contrasts and gradation of pace and emotion will depend on the overall view of the nature of the play. Crudely speaking, there are two possibilities, which we can call the 'psychological' and the 'ritual'. It is of these that Roland Barthes wrote in a fascinating review of a production of *Phèdre*, where he speaks of 'l'embarras visible des acteurs et du public devant un théâtre que l'on veut traiter à la fois comme une comédie psychologique et comme un oratorio'. The difficulty will arise in relation to the question of tempo; it arises most clearly, however, in the choice of a style of speaking: 'dans un langage aussi "distant" que celui de la tragédie classique, le choix de la diction domine de très haut le choix de l'interprétation' (*Sur Racine*, pp. 136–9).

Diction

Most theatrical dialogue is poised between a life-like imitation of real speech and the creation of a deliberately stylized alternative to it. Verse drama poses the problem in a particularly acute form. If one looks at *Andromaque* as a stage in the development of theatrical dialogue in France, one notices how far it has moved towards a credible imitation of natural speech as compared with the openly oratorical tragedy of the sixteenth century or even the exciting yet formal exchanges which fill the earlier tragedies of Racine's old rival, Pierre Corneille. Compare the following passages, dating respectively from 1640 and 1667:

CURIACE

> Que désormais le ciel, les enfers et la terre
> Unissent leurs fureurs à nous faire la guerre;
> Que les hommes, les dieux, les démons et le sort
> Préparent contre nous un général effort:
> Je mets à faire pis, en l'état où nous sommes,
> Le sort, et les démons, et les dieux, et les hommes.
> Ce qu'ils ont de cruel, et d'horrible, et d'affreux,
> L'est bien moins que l'honneur qu'on nous fait à tous deux.
>
> (Corneille, *Horace*, II. iii)

PYRRHUS

> Rien ne vous engageait à m'aimer en effet.

HERMIONE

> Je ne t'ai point aimé, cruel? Qu'ai-je donc fait?
> J'ai dédaigné pour toi les vœux de tous nos princes.
> Je t'ai cherché moi-même au fond de tes provinces;
> J'y suis encor, malgré tes infidélités,
> Et malgré tous mes Grecs honteux de mes bontés.
> Je leur ai commandé de cacher mon injure;
> J'attendais en secret le retour d'un parjure;
> J'ai cru que tôt ou tard, à ton devoir rendu,
> Tu me rapporterais un coeur qui m'était dû.
> Je t'aimais inconstant, qu'aurais-je fait fidèle?
> Et même en ce moment où ta bouche cruelle
> Vient si tranquillement m'annoncer le trépas,
> Ingrat, je doute encor si je ne t'aime pas.
> Mais, Seigneur, s'il le faut, si le ciel en colère
> Réserve à d'autres yeux la gloire de vous plaire,
> Achevez votre hymen, j'y consens. Mais du moins
> Ne forcez pas mes yeux d'en être les témoins.
> Pour la dernière fois je vous parle peut-être:
> Différez-le d'un jour; demain vous serez maître.
> Vous ne répondez point? Perfide, je le voi,
> Tu comptes les moments que tu perds avec moi! . . .   (IV.v)

These are of course extreme examples. Corneille only rarely writes
with quite so extravagant a flourish, whereas in *Andromaque* we can find
many examples of speeches more obviously oratorical than that of

Hermione. Even so, the comparison brings out quite clearly the extent to which Racine is moulding the classical alexandrine to what we may perhaps accept as a stylized version of real speech patterns. The passage from *Horace* is the reaction of a man to the sort of announcement which leaves one (as they say) speechless. Corneille shapes his alexandrines with four echoing sets of three terms distributed over four equally weighted rhyming couplets in order to give a powerful and in modern terms 'unrealistic' expression to this speechless horror. If it moves the spectator, it is in the manner of opera rather than of naturalistic drama. Hermione's speech is different. It too is an expression of unbearable emotion, coming at the end of the tense scene (IV.v) in which Pyrrhus has come to declare his changed intention to the woman who loves him. The spectators know as they watch it that, although she still loves Pyrrhus, Hermione has sent Oreste to kill him, and until this point have sensed her emotions half-concealed behind a front of bitterly ironical politeness. Only here, at the end of the scene, does the feeling break through the mask.

First there is the famous *tutoiement*, the shift from *vous* to *tu* that we find at so many crises of seventeenth-century tragedy. The first line, quite unlike the traditional tragic alexandrine, is broken into two unequal parts, each of which is an insistent rhetorical question. Then come a series of sentences which can be spoken so as to give an impression of breathless accumulation. At first there is a break at the end of nearly every line, and only after several lines does the sense extend to a more measured sentence of three lines. This is the signal for a return to *vous* and a desperate attempt to return to a calmer tone—a bid to prevent Pyrrhus's immediate marriage with Andromaque. But the control soon breaks, the sentences grow shorter and the passionate *tutoiement* reappears, fracturing once again the regular rhythm of the alexandrine.

The contrasts and gradation which mark the syntax and speech rhythms is visible too in the shifts of vocabulary. Hermione's first line is basic French; then, as her speech gathers momentum, she comes back to something more like the conventional language of love in seventeenth-century literature ('les vœux de tous nos princes', 'mes bontés', 'un parjure', 'un cœur qui m'était dû', 'le trépas'), and this in turn is followed by a distinctly elaborate and figurative sentence as she tries to return to calm reasoning ('si le ciel en colère . . .'), only to revert to the simplicity of 'Tu comptes les moments que tu perds avec moi.'

One can see how much scope such a speech gives to a 'psychological' rendering, in which the actress makes the most of all Racine's lines, sacrificing the regularity of the verse to the continual and violent flux of emotion, alternating shouts and breathless pauses with passages of deliberate and tactical formality. It is possible that Racine himself encouraged his actors and actresses to play in this way; his son Louis wrote that Hermione's last words should be said with the following pauses:

> Adieu—tu peux partir—je demeure en Epire—
> Je renonce—à la Grèce—à Sparte—à ton empire—
> A toute ta famille—et c'est assez pour moi
> Traître—qu'elle ait produit un monstre—comme toi. (V.iii)

But there are anecdotes which work the other way. The actors of the Hôtel de Bourgogne company, who first performed most of Racine's tragedies, were sometimes mocked for their heavy style, and a few years after *Andromaque* it was maliciously claimed that they were infringing Lully's operatic monopoly by singing their lines. There is no doubt that many elements in Racine's language work against any sort of naturalistic performance. If a naturalistic style brings the audience closer to the dramatic action, then these other elements are likely to make us keep our distance and see in Racine's plays a noble ceremony rather than an image of life as we know it.

In the first place, the speech of Racine's people is almost always well formed, and makes full use of all the patterns of symmetry, repetition and enumeration which are the mark of formal oratory. This is naturally the case when Pyrrhus and Oreste meet as king and ambassador, matching

> L'Épire sauvera ce que Troie a sauvé

against

> Hector tomba sous lui, Troie expira sous vous. (I.ii)

But it is also true in those more private scenes where individuals confront one another or unburden themselves to their confidants. Listen to Oreste as he begins to go mad:

> J'assassine à regret un roi que je révère;
> Je viole en un jour les droits des souverains,
> Ceux des ambassadeurs, et tous ceux des humains,
> Ceux même des autels où ma fureur l'assiège:
> Je deviens parricide, assassin, sacrilège.
> Pour qui? (V.iv)

It is not difficult here to detect the same patterns of formal rhetoric as in Oreste's ambassadorial speech. Similarly, at almost all points in the play, the element of oratory is balanced against that of 'normal' speech. Not that the two are rigorously opposed to one another; the figures of repetition and symmetry which combine so well with the alexandrine are already present in an embryonic form in our everyday language. So what we have here is a heightening of emotional speech into powerful theatrical declamation. It could be seen as a difference of degree, not of kind, and does not present the actor with any insuperable difficulty.

There is, however, a greater difficulty, and this is when speech is opposed not so much to oratory as to poetry or music. To start with, there is the obvious fact that *Andromaque* is written in a form of verse which will strike English audiences at least as unusually regular and ceremonious—cesuras, rhyming couplets, alternation of masculine and feminine rhymes. It is true that the alexandrine has no fixed pattern of stresses, so that the regular metre can be combined with immense rhythmic variation; any four consecutive lines in *Andromaque* are likely to show a different rhythmical pattern in each line. Nevertheless, the rhyming alexandrine, although considered as the tragic equivalent of prose by some of Racine's contemporaries, is constantly pulling the language away from that of normal speech.

This is accentuated by the maintenance of strict decorum, which excludes all the low expressions of comedy or satire and confines Racine to a basic 'noble' vocabulary of some two thousand words. Of these words a good number belong to the conventional figurative style of the time, *flamme* for love, *la fureur des eaux* for storm and so on. As we saw a moment ago, the use of this noble idiom may serve a psychological function when contrasted with plainer speaking, but it is also a sign that we are in a different world from that of every day, the world of theatrical ceremony.

Thus the same speech which can be spoken in a naturalistic way can also be savoured as poetry and well-nigh chanted. Take the following brief speech from a relatively minor character, Pylade:

> Allons, Seigneur, enlevons Hermione.
> Au travers des périls un grand cœur se fait jour.
> Que ne peut l'amitié conduite par l'amour?
> Allons de tous vos Grecs encourager le zèle.
> Nos vaisseaux sont tout prêts, et le vent nous appelle.

Je sais de ce palais tous les détours obscurs;
Vous voyez que la mer en vient battre les murs;
Et cette nuit, sans peine, une secrète voie
Jusqu'en votre vaisseau conduira votre proie. (III.i)

These words tell us of Pylade's capitulation to Oreste's purpose, and with repeated imperatives they move the action towards some sort of outcome; they also inform both Oreste and the spectator of the lie of the land. But they do other things too. The second and third lines, for instance, are both maxims which can be spoken in such a way that they stand slightly apart from the movement of the speech, echoing one another. The first of them contains a complex set of half-perceived figures, 'cœur' being taken for courage and 'au travers' and 'se fait jour' suggesting some such action as breaking out of a labyrinth or a thicket. In the second (disguised as a question) the abstract nouns 'amitié' and 'amour' are personified and appear fleetingly as figures in some allegorical painting. The fourth line returns to the exhortation of the beginning, but the apparently practical fifth line goes beyond mere information. The symmetry of the alexandrine, with the echoing initial 'v' of 'vaisseaux' and 'vent' and the similarity of sound between 'prêts' and 'appelle', briefly sets the mind free of the immediate situation, encouraging the imagination to dwell for an instant on the sea as a place of freedom, a refuge from the murderous palace. The powerful and suggestive image of sea and palace is reinforced by the four lines that follow, lines which gain some of their impact from the relative rarity of such visual evocation in the play as a whole.

Such a combination of perception transcending the immediate situation and pleasure in sound and image can be generated at many points in the play, but it is most clearly called for by some of the words of Andromaque, since her eyes are principally fixed on the abolished past (Hector) or the unrealized future (Astyanax). When she describes herself in a much-quoted line as

Captive, toujours triste, importune à moi-même (I.iv)

she is arguing with Pyrrhus, dissuading him from pressing her to marry him; but at the same time her words can be spoken so as to float free of her debate with Pyrrhus, defining her for ever as an image of grief ('like Niobe, all tears'). The line is the more noticeable for being isolated syntactically from the sentence to which it belongs; it is placed in apposition *before* the main clause and relates (incorrectly, grammarians might say) to the subject of the subordinate clause, not the main clause:

> Captive, toujours triste, importune à moi-même,
> Pouvez-vous souhaiter qu'Andromaque vous aime?

It also impresses itself on the memory by virtue of the famous *musique racinienne* of which it has so often been taken as an example. What is meant by *musique* here?

Primarily, I think, it is that having heard it, one wants to repeat it again and again, dwelling on it as on a favourite tune, no longer thinking principally of what it means (though this is not lost) but laying oneself open to the appeal of sound patterns which can only partly be analysed. The succession of three units of increasing length is probably important—the first and second units are both of three syllables, but 'toujours triste' with its full syllables, its two words and its place before the cesura carries more weight than 'captive'. Then there is the combination of repetition and variety in the arrangement of vowels and consonants—the numerous 't' sounds at the beginning set against the three 'm's at the end, the 'p-t' group that appears near the beginning of each hemistich, the two 'ou' sounds coming between the two 'i' sounds in the first hemistich, the contrast between the repeated vowels in the first hemistich and the five different vowels in the second (*moi* rhymes with 'a' in modern pronunciation, with 'e' in seventeenth-century pronunciation). Such patterns are not beautiful or significant in themselves, any more than the music of Mozart, but in our culture people have come to regard them as such and to value a performance of *Andromaque* which does justice to the sensual aspect of Racine's language. This ought to mean not so much a highlighting of anthology pieces as a constant awareness of what for short we can call the poetic side to Racine's tragedy.

In the pull between poetic and psychological diction we can see a formal expression of the problem of distance and closeness which I mentioned at the outset. The desire to bring Racine closer may tempt producers to ignore the alexandrine and its music, the attempt to be faithful to the oratorical or poetic nature of French classical tragedy may lead them to iron out the human appeal of a play such as *Andromaque*. Can the circle be squared? Can the poetic and the psychological coexist? If not, how should one choose between them? It is very unsatisfactory to discuss in the abstract the speaking of Racine's verse; one needs to attend different performances or listen to different recordings in order to compare solutions and see what overall view of the play they serve; or perhaps best of all one can try speaking it oneself. It is probably better to start by saying the lines as neutrally as possible and let the emphasis emerge gradually, rather than try to impose from the outset some notion of Racinian passion or Racinian music. But it remains a problem, and one that is not often solved to the spectator's satisfaction.

The Visual Aspect

French classical tragedy is often described as predominantly verbal; a critic of the time said that in the theatre 'parler, c'est agir.' Nevertheless, we do not usually talk of going to 'hear' *Andromaque*. In an actual theatrical production the visual is extremely important, and even when the play is read or heard, it calls on us to imagine, if only vaguely, some sort of physical presence. What sort?

Choice of costume and set may be related to decisions about the style of speaking. It is possible, but not easy, to produce *Andromaque* in modern dress, alexandrines and all. It is also possible to cover the actors' faces in heavy masks. Normal seventeenth-century tragic dress was what we should now consider an odd mixture of ancient and contemporary elements, the whole conventionally signifying 'tragic antiquity'. Most producers today work equally within a convention, though modern costuming and sets usually stress historical accuracy more than did Racine's contemporaries; where they set their action in a generalized palace with a few statues (*un palais à volonté*), modern producers may be more inclined to look for something that impresses the spectator as genuinely Greek. Since Racine's day there has been a great increase in people's awareness of historical change and of the specificity of different periods, so that *Andromaque* confronts us at once with fragmentary images of two alien societies, Homeric Greece and Racine's France. Either or both of these may affect the way a modern production looks.

Then we have electric light. In Racine's day there was no possibility of varying the lighting and although the stage was more brightly lit than the auditorium, there was no rigid separation between darkened auditorium and brightly lit stage. If we make this separation, it may work to set off the actors as figures in a remote and glamorous pageant, but conversely, as in the cinema, it may encourage a more intense imaginative identification between actor and spectator. Modern lighting also makes it possible to point up the rhythm or significance of the action—for instance, rather crudely, by flooding the stage in darkness as Oreste loses his reason.

These are only a few remarks to indicate some of the variables that go to create the total physical spectacle. Like the choice of diction, they depend on the producer's guiding conception of the play and its meaning. Even more closely related to diction is the question of gesture and movement. Racine's play has virtually no stage directions. Does that mean that one is to aim at a sort of verbal ritual where people move as little as possible, or should one fill out the words with the kinds of movement which make more explicit the emotions and tensions one wishes to convey?

Take Act I, Scene iv. In psychological terms the essence of this scene lies in Pyrrhus's repeated attempts to persuade Andromaque, threatening and pleading by turns. The initiative is all on his side, her part is to parry his advances, finding counter-arguments and sometimes resorting to aggression as the best defence. Since she tells him in her first lines that she is simply on her way to see her son, one could imagine her remaining in a fixed position, fighting off his attacks, but turning her eyes all the time to the far distance, to her son, her husband, and the 'sacrés murs' of Troy. Pyrrhus meanwhile would be full of movement, circling round her, getting at her literally from all angles, and matching the extravagant energy of his talk with his gestures and facial expressions. The scene would then be a contrast between her noble immobility and his feverish attempts to thrust himself on her, physically as well as morally. Alternatively, though, she could be seen meeting gesture with gesture and physically advancing on him at such points as 'Et pourquoi vos soupirs seraient-ils repoussés?'; this would create a quite different scene in which two antagonists do battle with equal weapons.

However a scene such as this is played, good modern productions of Racine often make a good deal of the physical confrontation of characters such as Pyrrhus and Andromaque, showing through 'body language' their mutual attraction, repulsion, hostility or indifference. It is hard to tell from the surviving evidence what Racine's original actors did. It seems unlikely that they touched one another—even today this is not common in productions of Racine—but it is quite probable that they used a formal system of gesture to convey emotions and attitudes. The original frontispiece to *Andromaque* (by F. Chauveau) shows a scene between Andromaque and Pyrrhus in which she is kneeling and holding out both hands in a gesture of supplication; Céphise too is kneeling, but wringing her hands, while Pyrrhus is standing with his body half turned away from her but his head looking down at her and his right hand outstretched over her head. Of course this illustration may merely follow the codes of gesture which regulated seventeenth-century painting, and may bear little resemblance to actual stage production, but it is certainly suggestive.

Of one thing one can be fairly certain, however, and this is that the face and eyes were important for Racine's actors. *Andromaque* is full of references to the eyes, which are seen as a vital means of communication, enabling people to dominate one another or to show their mutual affection or indifference. Pyrrhus says to Andromaque:

> Mais parmi ces périls où je cours pour vous plaire,
> Me refuserez-vous un regard moins sévère? (I.iv)

Hermione in her turn seeks Pyrrhus' eyes and fails to find them:

> Perfide, je le voi,
> Tu comptes les moments que tu perds avec moi!
> Ton cœur, impatient de revoir ta Troyenne,
> Ne souffre qu'à regret qu'un autre t'entretienne.
> Tu lui parles du cœur, tu la cherches des yeux. (IV.v)

But she too has her victim, Oreste, who exclaims

> Je sais que vos regards vont rouvrir mes blessures. (II.ii)

We may perhaps take Oreste's words merely as a part of his conventional lover's language, but I think the power of Hermione's eyes can also be shown physically, and certainly the words of Pyrrhus and Hermione can be acted on as concealed stage directions. The way the actors look at one another can do a great deal to reinforce the portrayal of their emotional relationships, but here again, it all depends how far the producer wants to take the psychological realism of the production.

Character

Those reading Racine's plays at school or university are sometimes asked to do 'character studies' of stage figures such as Hermione or Oreste. Similarly, those who write about Racine will often feel it necessary to draw out the 'character' of the main protagonists—Racine himself was the first to do this when he discussed Pyrrhus and Andromaque in the two prefaces he wrote for his play. Producers and

A 3173

actors too will try to define for themselves and the audience the nature of the protagonists, and readers do something of the sort as they read the words on the page. It cannot be too strongly stressed, however, that these characters are not 'there', they are what we create out of the verbal material that Racine has given us. Racine may have had an unequivocal idea about the sort of people he had created, but he is no longer there to tell us—it is up to us to interpret. Not that the details of this interpretation are necessarily very important. If we hold to something like the 'ritual' view of Racine's tragedy suggested above in the section on diction, the actors may be regarded more as figures performing a function in a dramatic representation than as particular individuals with relationships of a particular kind and 'character' will be no more than a kind of interesting but inessential colouring. Even so, some choices are called for.

In a stage production the first act of interpretation comes with the casting. Actors may be chameleon-like, but they still make their personal mark on the characters they represent. It makes a difference, for instance, whether they are young or old, short or tall, beautiful or ugly. We read in a contemporary rhyming gazette that at the first performance Andromaque

> Se remontre, pleine d'appâts,
> Sous le visage d'une actrice,
> Des humains grande tentatrice . . .
> C'est Mademoiselle Du Parc.

The actress's appearance and reputation seem in this case to have suggested a seductive, coquettish Andromaque—not quite what most readers see in the part today.

Even if a producer had total freedom to choose the actors he wanted and direct them as he desired, it is by no means obvious what he should aim for. Let us take Pyrrhus as an example. Racine gives us some indications about this character in his preface: 'J'avoue qu'il n'est pas assez résigné à la volonté de sa maîtresse. . . . Mais que faire? Pyrrhus n'avait pas lu nos romans. Il était violent de son naturel.' But these remarks only create confusion, since Racine is here giving an oblique answer to critics who accused him of the opposite fault, that of making Pyrrhus an excessively polite lover. And if we look at what Pyrrhus says and does in the play and at what the other characters say about him, we find a bewildering set of contradictions. There is the brutal murderer of Priam and Polyxenes, and the noble king who answers Oreste in Act I, Scene ii;

there is the cool and polite Pyrrhus who faces Hermione in Act IV, Scene v and the distraught figure of Act I, Scene iv, the potentially comic lover who cannot hide his love from Phoenix, and the tragic victim of the last act. In part these contradictions correspond to the different moods of the other characters; what Hermione sees as charming exploits in Act III, Scene iii, she can present as degraded bestiality in Act IV, Scene v. And in any case we can say that this sort of oscillation between strength and weakness, generosity and meanness, is precisely what makes up Pyrrhus's character; Pylade says of him in the opening scene:

> Ainsi n'attendez pas que l'on puisse aujourd'hui
> Vous répondre d'un cœur si peu maître de lui.

Even so, though we may agree that Pyrrhus is volatile and unreliable, there can still be very different images of him. When he says to Andromaque at the beginning of Act I, Scene iv:

> Me cherchiez-vous, Madame?
> Un espoir si charmant me serait-il permis?

should he be portrayed as a charmingly naïve and vulnerable young man, or as a cynical tyrant who is about to submit his victim to a piece of heartless blackmail? There is no right answer to the question. We cannot even give him the sort of precise age which a playwright such as Ibsen attaches to his characters before the first scene.

Our image of Racine's heroes is often greatly influenced by their previous existence in legend and literature. For readers of Virgil, Pyrrhus is above all the fierce and bloody man evoked by Book II of the *Aeneid*, 'in all his insolent glory' and 'crazed with blood lust', the figure depicted some sixty years before *Andromaque* in the Senecan pastiche in *Hamlet*

> horridly tricked
> With blood of fathers, mothers, daughters, sons,
> Baked and impasted with the parching streets.

One can understand why some of Racine's first spectators saw a contradiction between the Pyrrhus of legend and the man we see at certain points in *Andromaque*.

All the main characters in the play carry with them a similarly rich set of associations deriving from Homer, Virgil and other writers of antiquity. Racine had to take this into account in creating his heroes—thus he explains in his second preface how he has chosen out of the possible images of Andromaque the one which best fits the general view: 'La plupart de ceux qui ont entendu parler d'Andromaque, ne la connaissent guère que pour la veuve d'Hector et pour la mère d'Astyanax.' This would suggest that the actress playing Andromaque should conform to the traditional noble image of grief. But even here there are other possibilities. In the version of the play first performed in 1667, Racine had Andromaque reappearing after Pyrrhus's death and proclaiming her loyalty to her second husband. On the strength of this and other passages where she seems to speak of Pyrrhus with some degree of sympathy or admiration, a producer or actress might attempt to show that Andromaque is 'really' more attracted to Pyrrhus that she will admit. Thus in Act I, Scene iv, Andromaque needles Pyrrhus with a number of taunts. The common-sense reading of this is that she is trying to shame Pyrrhus into giving up his suit and at the same time giving vent to her hate for him, but knowing how close love and hate can be in Racine, one could perhaps read these taunts as signs that Andromaque is paradoxically drawn to Pyrrhus. Numerous scholars have condemned this reading as perverse and novelettish, and I am rather inclined to agree with them, but in saying so one is doing no more than stating the majority opinion: here again it is up to producers and readers to do what they can within the considerable margin of freedom left by Racine.

In the case of Oreste, the heritage of antiquity is almost embarrassing. Orestes was principally famous in legend for killing his mother Clytemnestra; it was for this reason that he was depicted as 'tristis Orestes', pursued by the Furies. In Racine's play he conforms fairly closely to this melancholy type, and there is probably no real debate about the sort of person the actor should represent. What is left ambiguous, however, is his past. Has he already killed Clytemnestra or is he still a young man with a terrible future? Interpretations have differed. The play contains no reference to the murder of Clytemnestra, and the dating of the action (about one year after the Trojan War) seems to rule out the possibility that the deed is already done. And yet the gloomy Oreste bears all the marks of the legendary criminal, and is even given the traditional vision of the Furies in the last scene.

The other characters offer fewer problems of interpretation. There can be little doubt that Hermione will be played as young and passionate, capable of furious action, but also of icy restraint, by turns self-deceiving and terribly aware of what is going on. Even so, it is not possible to assign precise motives to her words and actions; her love for Pyrrhus is presented as an inextricable fusion of sexual attraction and the vulnerable pride that surfaces in such lines as

> Quelle honte pour moi, quel triomphe pour lui,
> De voir mon infortune égaler son ennui! (II.i)

Every Hermione will be different, varying from the attractively impulsive to the repellingly egoistic. Moreover, she is one element in a set of four main actors; in this set we perceive people in an interrelated way, often contrasted with one another, so that if Pyrrhus is made to seem particularly unpleasant, Hermione and Andromaque are likely to win more sympathy—and vice versa.

The confidants too play their part in this web of relationships. These advisers, friends, governors and ladies-in-waiting are often thought of as mere utilities in French classical tragedy, but in fact they are on stage for a large part of the action and they can be formidable presences. Thus in Roger Planchon's splendid production of *Bérénice* the emperor Titus was reduced to an insubstantial boy by his confidant Paulin, who appeared as the all-too-solid embodiment of Roman politics. Something similar can be imagined in *Andromaque*. Pylade's loyalty and common sense act primarily as a foil to set off the emotional twists and turns of his friend Oreste, but he may also be played as the dominant partner, much as in comedy a cool-headed servant can lead a headstrong young master. (It is interesting that Racine has made him address Oreste as 'vous', while Oreste calls him 'tu', thus suggesting that he is Oreste's social inferior rather than the true friend of legend.) Pylade is there at the beginning and end—he does not live at tragic pitch and he survives.

The other confidants probably give less scope for the creation of character; as with Pylade, their role is partly to provoke confidences, but also to argue vainly in favour of practical self-interested behaviour. Even so, it is possible to allow them considerable power over their masters and mistresses. The most striking example is Act II, Scene v, where the teasing reproaches of Phoenix make Pyrrhus look both comic and childish. It seems likely that the separation of tragedy from comedy would not have allowed the comic potential of this scene to be realized in Racine's day, but modern productions have shown that it is there. The barrier between the genres is at the same time rigid and fragile.

This brief consideration of characters should have made it clear that *Andromaque* is a shifting mosaic in which producers and actors can exert a great influence on one's understanding of the play. Both the balance of interest or sympathy and the portrayal of individual protagonists can differ considerably from one production to another. Maurice Descotes's interesting book *Les Grande Roles dans le théâtre de Racine* shows how the interpretation of the major parts has varied from age to age and how certain actors and actresses have seemed to embody particular characters for their generation. What is more, memories of stage productions, films or even photographs influence our conception of the characters and the play as we read in solitude. But in solitary reading we are freed from the producer's obligation to choose between conflicting images. As with diction, we can have it several ways at once.

3. Text and Meaning

Reading a play is a very different business from going to the theatre. True, the reader often attempts to imagine a theatrical production, and conversely the spectator may try to 'read' and understand a play during performance. But real reading gives the opportunity to stop and go back, to look at the text in different ways, to reflect on detail, to dwell on similarities and contrasts, and to take pleasure in the texture of the language. It may also provoke us to search out a meaning.

'Meaning' is an awkward word to use about literature. There is an eighteenth-century story of a mathematician who came out of a play by Racine asking: 'What does it prove?' And of course *Andromaque* does not prove anything. It would in my view be an illusion to suppose that there is some organic unity of meaning or vision in a play which we can get at by careful and sympathetic reading. What is true, I think, is that a play such as this, particularly when read and discussed, provokes all sorts of questions, and this questioning may goad the reader into *constructing* some overall meaning or meanings to make sense of the complicated and often fragmented experience of reading. In this chapter I shall try to draw out some of the strands which we can weave together in our reading of the play.

A Vision of Humanity: 'Misère' and 'Grandeur'

If the playing of individual characters leaves so much room for choice, so too will the overall view of humanity which we can gather from the pages of *Andromaque*. Let us begin with the most dismal reading.

At no point in the play is there any free and equal communication between people. Even Oreste and Pylade, who come down from antiquity as the model of friendship, are separated by the gap between *tu* and *vous* and by their quite different cast of mind. Once perhaps they were true friends, but now Oreste is picked out by fate and dedicated to suicidal passion, while Pylade remains devoted to the familiar values of loyalty, self-respect and self-preservation. Oreste cuts short his friend's sensible advice:

> Non, tes conseils ne sont plus de saison,
> Pylade, je suis las d'écouter la raison. (III.i)

So too all the main protagonists neglect the pragmatic help of their confidants, choosing to live in their own tragic world. The near-comic scene between Pyrrhus and Phoenix (II.v) is echoed in a more moving way by the scenes in which Andromaque rejects the well-meant advice of Céphise (III.viii and IV.i).

At least between confidant and hero there is the bond of loyalty. The four heroes, however, confront one another across gulfs of hostile incomprehension. A characteristic form of this *dialogue de sourds* is the scene in which one person talks eloquently into a void, since the other's mind is fixed elsewhere—thus Pyrrhus to Andromaque in Act I, Scene iv, Oreste to Hermione in Act II, Scene ii and Act IV, Scene iii, Andromaque to Hermione in Act III, Scene iv, Hermione to Pyrrhus at the end of Act IV, Scene v and finally, once again, Pylade to Oreste in the concluding scene.

Never do two protagonists really want the same thing. It is not enough, however, for them to ignore what is being said to them; such disdain is only possible from a position of security, but all the people here are insecure, all have something to obtain from someone else. So in Act III, Scene vi, which begins like a comic *dépit amourex*, Andromaque and Pyrrhus are forced by their different desires to abandon their silence and enter into a sort of relationship. Two clusters of metaphor stand out as ways of describing human relationships in *Andromaque*—trade and war.

In speaking of trade, I am thinking of Hermione, Pyrrhus, Oreste and Andromaque as coming into a market-place with certain assets or debts, and certain ends in view; from a position of total selfishness they will make the most of their assets, seek to evade their debts, trick one another and resort to theft if need be. Hermione has come to Epirus with a claim on Pyrrhus which makes him an 'ingrat' in her eyes; when he appears willing to honour the contract she says disingenuously to Oreste:

> Lui ravirai-je un bien qu'il ne tient pas de moi?

The notion of an irksome debt of gratitude appears again when Pyrrhus accuses Andromaque:

> Vous craignez de devoir quelque chose à ma flamme.

Andromaque in her turn regards Astyanax as 'le seul bien qui me reste' and is willing to marry Pyrrhus in order to place him in her debt and oblige him to protect her son. Similarly, Oreste finally agrees to kill Pyrrhus in order to earn Hermione, only to be robbed of his salary:

> Et l'ingrate, en fuyant, me laisse pour salaire
> Tous les noms odieux que j'ai pris pour lui plaire! (V.iv)

There are many more passages where similar words appear: *bien*, *ravir*, *ingrat*, *salaire*, *payer*, *devoir*, *récompense*, *droit*, *acheter*. In this market-place there is no room for generosity. As Andromaque says to Pyrrhus, the truly generous person would.

> Sauver des malheureux, rendre un fils à sa mère,
> De cent peuples pour lui combattre la rigueur,
> Sans me faire payer son salut de mon cœur. (I.iv)

But she is wasting her breath; nothing is given for nothing in this world.

The second group of metaphors is much more obvious—those evoking violent physical conflict, torture, war and conquest. The burning of Troy and the massacre of the Trojans are a model of inhumanity; such images of horror are forced on the reader, most memorably in Andromaque's speeches of Act III, Scenes vi and viii, and provide a physical parallel for the mental cruelty that fills the play. Pyrrhus makes the connection explicit when he compares his own brutality at Troy to what he describes as Andromaque's cruelty:

> J'ai fait des malheureux, sans doute; et la Phrygie
> Cent fois de votre sang a vu ma main rougie.
> Mais que vos yeux sur moi se sont bien exercés!

and so on, with a plethora of fires and chains, to

> Hélas! fus-je jamais si cruel que vous l'êtes! (I.iv)

Perhaps Pyrrhus is the ham actor here, deceiving himself with his own eloquence, just as Oreste compares Hermione's 'cruelty' to that of the Scythians and is cut down to size by her reply:

Quittez, Seigneur, quittez ce funeste langage. (II.ii)

But this 'funeste langage', misused as it is by the two men, is entirely apt
for the relations of hostility and domination that fill the play. Even if the
adjectives 'cruelle' and 'inhumaine' sit uneasily on Andromaque, she too
is drawn into the hostilities, parrying Pyrrhus' advances with the bitter
irony of

> Un enfant malheureux, qui ne sait pas encor
> Que Pyrrhus est son maître, et qu'il est fils d'Hector (I.iv)

or the ferocity of

> Et vous n'êtes tous deux connus que par mes larmes. (I.iv)

Then in Act IV she finds a 'stratagème' to cheat Pyrrhus, reminding us
perhaps of the earlier stratagem used at Troy to save her son

> Tandis qu'un autre enfant, arraché de ses bras,
> Sous le nom de son fils fut conduit au trépas. (I.i)

Towards this nameless child Andromaque too has been guilty of
inhumanity.

Her 'cruelty', however, appears mild compared to that of the other
characters. The vindictiveness of the Greeks at Troy is echoed by the
sadistic rage of Oreste or Hermione's desire to humiliate her rival:

> Rendons-lui les tourments qu'elle me fait souffrir. (II.i)

In the constant struggle for power the victors, like the warriors of the
Iliad, take pleasure in taunting their defeated enemies. Even when this
deliberate cruelty is apparently absent, the victims are able to imagine it;
in Act IV, Scene v it seems improbable that Pyrrhus has come to glory in
Hermione's misery, but that is how she interprets his intentions:

> Vous veniez de mon front observer la pâleur,
> Pour aller dans ses bras rire de ma douleur.
> Pleurante après son char vous voulez qu'on me voie.

In the absence of an external tormentor Racine's heroes and heroines are
adept at the self-torture that comes from wounded pride, unanswered
love and self-reproach.

For Hermione, Pyrrhus and Oreste, if not Andromaque, are all aware
of themselves as in some way degraded, and can feel the eyes of the world
on them as they fail to act their proper parts. Pyrrhus appears in Act I,

Scene ii, as a fine kingly figure, but before the act is over he is much
diminished. The public figure has given way to a frantic individual who
oscillates between extravagant eloquence and blackmail and knows
himself to be dependent on his so-called slave. In Act II, Scene v we see
him striving to live up to his kingly image, preening himself in the mirror
of Phoenix's admiration, but then slipping helplessly and ridiculously
back into his obsession. And in any case the heroic image which so pleases
Phoenix is itself cause for self-reproach, being founded primarily on the
murder of the innocent and defenceless, 'la vieillesse et l'enfance'.
Hermione's irony ('Que peut-on refuser à ces généreux coups?') seems to
go home, and provokes him to a counter-attack. It is hard to say whether
he should be seen as genuinely remorseful for this past, but at all events he
is forced by both Hermione and Andromaque to see himself as less than
the glorious 'vainqueur de Troie' whom Oreste had flattered in the first
act.

What makes matters worse is that these heroes and heroines are
descended from the magnificent figures of legend, Achilles, Agamemnon
and Helen. Magnificent, that is, not in themselves (Racine himself will
later show both Achilles and Agamemnon as far from perfect figures in
his *Iphigénie*), but in the minds of their children. Again and again, starting
with the list of *dramatis personae*, this heritage is brought before us, and the
protagonists themselves are oppressed by their failure to live up to their
family name. Hermione, whose 'orgueil' is at least equal to her love,
exclaims bitterly:

> Quoi? sans qu'elle employât une seule prière,
> Ma mère en sa faveur arma la Grèce entière? . . .
> Et moi, je ne prétends que la mort d'un parjure . . .
> Je me livre moi-méme, et ne puis me venger? (V.ii)

The young Oreste, who has missed the Trojan War, also feels the need to
match his father's reputation:

> Prenons, en signalant mon bras et votre nom,
> Vous, la place d'Hélène, et moi, d'Agamemnon.
> De Troie en ce pays réveillons les misères,
> Et qu'on parle de nous ainsi que de nos pères. (IV.iii)

But where Agamemnon had been the King of Kings, Pylade's verdict
on Oreste is dismissive:

> Voilà donc le succès qu'aura votre ambassade:
> Oreste ravisseur! (III.i)

One aspect of the degradation of these heroes is their ability to twist the meaning of words, to speak of justice and innocence when their actions or emotions seem to call for very different words. It is as if they could not ignore a standard of magnanimity or virtue which they cannot attain in practice—in the words of La Rochefoucauld, 'l'hypocrisie est un hommage que le vice rend à la vertu.' Andromaque presents her deceit as an 'innocent stratagème', Oreste describes Hermione as 'un bien qu'il m'a ravi' when he, Oreste, is in fact the 'ravisseur', Phoenix talks of Pyrrhus's 'heureuse cruauté' and 'juste courroux'. Words are a means of deceiving oneself and other people. They show too how these distracted people lose control of themselves, whether in the rhetorical extravagance of Oreste talking to Hermione, or in the confusion and bad faith with which Hermione makes Oreste responsible for Pyrrhus's death. Critics have often talked about the lucidity of Racine's characters, but such lucidity as they have is usually combined with a blindness and confusion bordering on madness. What we call madness actually invades the stage in the last scene, but long before this Oreste has been beside himself, out of his mind; as Pylade says:

Je ne vous connais plus: vous n'êtes plus vous-même. (III.i)

Like Oreste, Pyrrhus and Hermione are in an intermittent state of frenzy throughout the play, torn, divided, out of control.

Unloving, self-centred, possessive, violent, sadistic, self-tormenting, degenerate, dishonest, self-deceiving, mad—such is the vision of humanity I have so far drawn out of *Andromaque*. The tone of moral disapproval is perhaps inappropriate, and some readers have in fact argued that Racine is morally neutral. One can hardly fail to notice, however, that terms implying praise or blame—from 'généreux' to 'parricide' are always being used in the play, even if often in a confusing way. However much we sympathize with the characters in *Andromaque*, we cannot really avoid the implication that taken together they suggest a pretty gloomy image of the human race.

But is this black view the whole story? Does it apply equally to everyone in the play? Not to dwell on the confidants, who are at least faithful to their masters, mistresses or friends, can we not see among the main characters what René Hubert has called a 'moral hierarchy'? In particular, should we not say that Andromaque, who gives her name to the play, also provides a standard by which we can judge the others? Where they are selfish and aggressive, she is devoted to the memory of her husband and to her son; where they are confused and frenzied, she remains lucid and calm, the beautiful figure suggested by her opening words:

> Je passais jusqu'aux lieux où l'on garde mon fils.
> Puisqu'une fois le jour vous souffrez que je voie
> Le seul bien qui me reste et d'Hector et de Troie,
> J'allais, Seigneur, pleurer un moment avec lui!
> Je ne l'ai point encore embrassé d'aujourd'hui. (I.iv)

It is true that the circumstances of the play force her to defend her son, and so to show that she too can hate, fight, bargain, deceive and torment herself, but this is all sanctified by the cause of Hector and Astyanax. Essentially faithful to higher values, she embodies the refusal to accept life in a degraded world.

All of this is persuasive enough, though one may have doubts about the inherent goodness of the Trojan cause. But even if to most readers Andromaque does indeed represent a better kind of humanity than Pyrrhus, Oreste and Hermione, it is these other characters who dominate most of the play and who are likely to attract most of our interest and even sympathy. Neither does it seem right to lump them all together (as Lucien Goldmann did in *Le Dieu Caché*) as representatives of the 'inauthentic' world that Andromaque refuses. Pyrrhus in particular, for all his violence, weakness and confusion, can be seen as a positive force striving to escape from the horrors of the past (which paralyse Andromaque), confessing his former excesses and trying to make a new beginning. 'Violent mais sincère', noble and splendid in spite of his cruelty, he arguably comes nearer than any other figure in the play to Aristotle's idea of the tragic hero as Racine noted it: 'Il faut donc que ce soit un homme qui soit entre les deux, c'est-à-dire qui ne soit point extrêmement juste et vertueux, et qui ne mérite point aussi son malheur par un excès de méchanceté et d'injustice.' If there is greatness in Racine's vision of humanity, it can be seen in Pyrrhus as well as in Andromaque.

Indeed there is an element of greatness in all the main characters. Whatever one's moral judgement on even such a weak, impulsive, sadistic and self-pitying individual as Oreste is usually taken to be, he too is a 'hero' in the sense that he lives in the rarified and energetic world of Racine's tragic actors, not in the mundane sphere of the confidants. There is, in spite of everything, an aura of grandeur about these passionate, self-destroying people, as there is about Lady Macbeth and her husband. Oreste and Hermione are still the children of Agamemnon and Helen, they speak in splendid language, and they live with a special intensity. As one reads *Andromaque* one seems to receive a paradoxical view of humanity akin to that expressed in the words of Racine's near-contemporary Pascal: 'A mesure que les hommes ont de lumière, ils trouvent et grandeur et misère en l'homme.'

Reversal and Destiny

Aristotle saw reversal (*peripeteia*) as one of the most powerful springs of tragedy. The action of *Andromaque* is built round changes of fortunes—from good to bad, but also from bad to good. At its simplest, the play enacts the lesson of the Magnificat: 'He hath put down the mighty from their seats and hath exalted the humble and meek', and a good deal of its force derives from this most traditional of patterns.

In detail this reversal is most obvious in the favourite seventeenth-century paradox of the captive captor and the powerful slave. Andromaque sees herself as 'captive, toujours triste, importune à moi-même', but Pyrrhus knows better and contrasts her lot with that of Hermione:

> Le sort vous y voulut l'une et l'autre amener,
> Vous, pour porter des fers; elle, pour en donner.
> Cependant ai-je pris quelque soin de lui plaire?
> Et ne dirait-on pas, en voyant au contraire
> Vos charmes tout puissants et les siens dédaignés,
> Qu'elle est ici captive et que vous y régnez? (I.iv)

In the same scene the related theme of the warrior wounded by love is also stated at length by Pyrrhus:

> Je souffre tous les maux que j'ai faits devant Troie.

These themes are extremely common in seventeenth-century literature; what is more striking in *Andromaque* is the way actions and words are thrown out and return like uncontrolled boomerangs to strike down the thrower.

This sort of twist is also a familiar literary theme, similar to the dramatic irony of Sophocles's *Oedipus Rex*, where a clear-sighted and powerful hero launches a train of events which will leave him literally a blind beggar. In the previous section I spoke of the blindness of Racine's characters, their 'aveuglement funeste'; they do not know themselves or

one another, so whatever they do has unforeseen consequences. The wise
Pylade sees something of this when he advises Oreste:

> Plus on les veut brouiller, plus on va les unir.
> Pressez, demandez tout, pour ne rien obtenir. (I.i)

Oreste follows his advice, but the result is the opposite of what he had
hoped; Pyrrhus is apparently won over by his arguments and Oreste is
reduced to a state of frenzy—as Cléone says:

> Je le plains: d'autant plus qu'auteur de son ennui,
> Le coup qui l'a perdu n'est parti que de lui. (III.iii)

Then it is Hermione's turn to bring down disaster on herself; triumphing
in Pyrrhus' return, she taunts Andromaque:

> Vos yeux assez longtemps ont regné sur son âme.
> Faites-le prononcer: j'y souscrirai, Madame. (III.iii)

Andromaque does just this, and Hermione loses Pyrrhus.
   Pyrrhus meanwhile is intent on repudiating Andromaque, but in
talking to her he ruins his own plan:

> Oui, je sens à regret, qu'en excitant vos larmes,
> Je ne fais contre moi que vous donner des armes. (III.vii)

It is at the wedding ceremony, however, that he offers the clearest
example of classic blindness and *hubris*, like the king walking up the red
carpet to his death in Aeschylus's *Agamemnon*. This is how Cléone sees
him:

> Madame, il ne voit rien. Son salut et sa gloire
> Semblent être avec vous sortis de sa mémoire.
> Sans songer qui le suit, ennemis ou sujets,
> Il poursuit seulement ses amoureux projets. (V.ii)

The important theme of sacrifice and the words 'temple' and 'autel' are
closely associated with Pyrrhus's reversal of fortune. At Troy Pyrrhus
had killed the old king Priam at the altar, in Epirus he is ordered by the
Greeks to complete the sacrifice by killing Astyanax. Thus in Act III,
Scene vii he declares to Andromaque that he will take her and her son to
the temple

> Et là vous me verrez, soumis ou furieux,
> Vous couronner, Madame, ou le perdre à vos yeux.

By Act V, however, he is convinced that the altar is the place of marriage and coronation—and so it proves to be; but it also becomes the place of sacrifice, not now of Astyanax, but of Pyrrhus himself, transformed from executioner into victim. All this irony is impressed on the reader by the third scene of Act IV, where Oreste and Hermione drum in the notion of sacrifice:

> Laissez-moi vers l'autel conduire ma victime.

The final victims of self-inflicted calamity are Hermione and Oreste. Hermione, unable to understand herself or to tell love from hate, condemns Pyrrhus to death and herself to suicide. She cannot accept that she is the author of her own ruin and puts the blame on Oreste:

> Ne devais-tu pas lire au fond de ma pensée? (V.iii)

But of course this is just what he could not do, so he is left devastated by his own miscalculation, fully aware of all the guilt he has incurred:

> Je deviens parricide, assassin, sacrilège.
> Pour qui? Pour une ingrate, à qui je le promets,
> Qui même, s'il ne meurt, ne me verra jamais,
> Dont j'épouse la rage. Et quand je l'ai servie,
> Elle me redemande et son sang et sa vie! (V.iv)

These ironic reversals are only a part of an even more all-embracing theme of the play—the interplay of active and passive. In the midst of their activity, the heroes feel that other forces are acting on them; conversely the fatalist resignation they sometimes express does not prevent them from acting. The tension and excitement of *Andromaque*, as of many tragedies, is based precisely on this paradoxical coexistence of action and passion, hope and destiny. It is a double perspective that stands out very clearly in Pyrrhus's lines:

> L'un par l'autre entraînés, nous courons à l'autel,
> Nous jurer, malgré nous, un amour immortel. (IV.vi)

where the vigorous 'courir' and 'jurer' are set against the passivity of 'entraînés' and 'malgré nous'. Andromaque sees herself as the resigned victim of Greece, Achilles and Pyrrhus, but Céphise assures her in Act III, Scene viii:

> Je vous l'avais prédit, qu'en dépit de la Grèce,
> De votre sort encor vous seriez la maîtresse.

And eventually, after an unhoped-for turn of events for which she is
nevertheless indirectly responsible, she finds herself acting against all her
previous intentions and taking up the cause of Pyrrhus against the Greeks.

It is, however, in Oreste's words and actions that we see most clearly
the interweaving of active and passive. It is his arrival and his speech to
Pyrrhus which spark off the action and it is he who precipitates the final
catastrophe by leading his soldiers to murder Pyrrhus. Yet throughout
the play his words express the conviction that he has no initiative, but is
the plaything of other forces. The grammar of the opening lines suggests
something of this tension:

> Oui, puisque je retrouve un ami si fidèle,
> Ma fortune va prendre une face nouvelle;
> Et déjà son courroux semble s'être adouci,
> Depuis qu'elle a pris soin de nous rejoindre ici.
> Qui l'eût dit, qu'un rivage à mes vœux si funeste
> Présenterait d'abord Pylade aux yeux d'Oreste?
> Qu'après plus de six mois que je t'avais perdu,
> A la cour de Pyrrhus tu me serais rendu?

The relatively active 'je' of the first line is quickly replaced as the subject
by 'ma fortune' and 'son courroux', then 'rivage' becomes the subject,
and after a brief reappearance of 'je' (but governing the negative verb
'perdre') the subject disappears altogether in the passive verb of the final
line. In his answer Pylade expresses the same vision, in which human
beings are acted upon by 'le ciel', 'la fureur des eaux' and 'un destin plus
heureux'. And soon, in Oreste's long expository speech, we come across
the explicit juxtaposition of initiative and fate:

> Mais admire avec moi le sort dont la poursuite
> Me fait courir alors au piège que j'évite.

This might almost be taken as a motto for the whole play: man proposes,
something else disposes.

What is this 'something else'? Oreste is in no doubt: it is fate or heaven
or the cruel gods, terms that are interchangeable for him:

> Oui, je te loue, ô Ciel, de ta persévérance.
> Appliqué sans relâche au soin de me punir,
> Au comble des douleurs tu m'as fait parvenir.
> Ta haine a pris plaisir à former ma misère. (V.v)

This is a familiar enough notion from European tragedy—but it should perhaps be read primarily as a projection of Oreste's own personality. He is the one who is most inclined to blame his misfortune on this malicious external force, while the others speak much less of the gods or fate. When Pyrrhus speaks of

> Le sort dont les arrêts furent alors suivis (I.ii)

he is merely referring to the operation of chance in the drawing of lots, and when Hermione invokes 'ces dieux, ces justes dieux' (IV.v) she has in mind the ancient religious sanction guaranteeing the inviolability of oaths rather than any hostile destiny.

It seems to me rather pointless to debate whether the sources of disaster in *Andromaque* are predominantly external (fate, the gods) or internal (human passions). Racine himself changed his mind on this; Oreste's line:

> Je me livre en aveugle au transport qui m'entraîne

was altered in later editions to read:

> Je me livre en aveugle au destin qui m'entraîne. (I.i)

In either case human beings are seen as subject to irresistible forces. Sexual obsession, anger, envy and pride are some of the gods that govern their lives.

There is, however, another force which leads to disaster; this is the power of other people. As we have seen, the whole play is based on a chain of incompatibilities; in this chain each person is for the next a god to be worshipped or an oracle to be consulted, in other words a force over which they have no control. Thus Oreste to Hermione:

> le destin d'Oreste
> Est de venir sans cesse adorer vos attraits. (II.ii)

Hermione depends on Pyrrhus's decisions as he depends on his deity Andromaque:

> Pour savoir nos destins, j'irai vous retrouver. (I.iv)

And Andromaque in turn is driven to visit her oracle:

> Allons sur son tombeau consulter mon époux. (III.viii)

Whatever one thinks of the notion of cruel gods, Racine shows his people as possessing only the most limited freedom of manœuvre between the demands of their own natures and the actions of those on whom they

depend. To these must be added, as my last example shows, the weight of
the past.

The Trojan War

Andromaque is like an illustration of Marx's words: 'The tradition of all
the dead generations weighs like an incubus on the brain of the living.'
Again and again the reader's attention is called to the Trojan War and
particularly to the fall of the city. We are not allowed to forget that the
people in the play are not just private individuals but Trojans and Greeks.
Pyrrhus and Andromaque were both present at Troy and all the actors are
closely related to the main protagonists in the war: Hector, Achilles,
Agamemnon, Helen and Menelaus. Indeed it often seems as if the action
of *Andromaque* is a continuation of the war or another version of it.

> Qu'ils cherchent dans l'Epire une seconde Troie, (I.ii)

Pyrrhus defies the Greeks, and his words are echoed by Hermione:

> Qu'on fasse de l'Epire un second Ilion (II.ii)

and by Oreste:

> De Troie en ce pays réveillons les misères. (IV.iii)

This quite recent past (only one year away) lays direct obligations on
those who live in the present. Andromaque has the contradictory duties
of remaining faithful to Hector and preserving Astyanax, sole survivor of
the royal line:

> Reste de tant de rois sous Troie ensevelis. (I.i)

Oreste has the official duty of pressing for the liquidation of the Trojan
cause; Pyrrhus and Hermione are committed to marriage by the
battlefield agreement of Achilles and Menelaus. The tragedy arises
because these duties conflict with one another and with the actual desire
of the characters.

In comparison with the past, the future is only fleetingly imagined, but
the importance of Astyanax in the action, even if he never actually comes
on to the stage, is that he allows us to see beyond the day of the tragedy
into a possible future. Indeed, if one reads the part of Book Three of the
Aeneid to which Racine refers in his preface one is given a fuller picture of
this future, in which Andromaque marries a Trojan husband, Helenus,

and sets up a new Troy in Epirus. So although the action is restricted to the usual twenty-four hours, the reader can attempt to make sense of the events of this day as part of a larger historical process.

It has been argued, among others by J. D. Hubert in his *Essai d'exégèse racinienne* and by Michael Edwards in his *La Tragédie racinienne*, that we should understand *Andromaque* as the story of the revenge or restoration of Troy. In Act I of the play, Pyrrhus declares his confidence that the fallen city can be raised again:

> Votre Ilion encor peut sortir de sa cendre;
> Je puis, en moins de temps que les Grecs ne l'ont pris,
> Dans ses murs relevés couronner votre fils. (I.iv)

And even if Troy is not literally rebuilt, we learn in the last act that Pyrrhus has indeed recognized Astyanax as the 'roi des Troyens'. It is this change of sides that enrages the Greek soldiers and is the immediate cause of his death. Andromaque, however, in answer to his earlier offer, had shown no hope for the resurrection of Troy; her eyes are still fixed on the city, but hopelessly:

> Non, vous n'espérez plus de nous revoir encor,
> Sacrés murs, que n'a pu conserver mon Hector. (I.iv)

She instructs Céphise that Astyanax is not to look for a return to power:

> Qu'il ne songe plus, Céphise, à nous venger:
> Nous lui laissons un maître, il le doit ménager.
> Qu'il ait de ses aïeux un souvenir modeste:
> Il est du sang d'Hector, mais il en est le reste. (IV.i)

Nevertheless, she succeeds in saving her son, so that after Pyrrhus's death she is in a position to take over the leadership of Epirus. Together with all the subjects of Pyrrhus, who have followed their king in his change of loyalties, she is reported in the final scene to be driving the Greeks out of the city. So Hector, who has been consulted like a god at the play's turning point between Acts III and IV, finishes by having his revenge on the Greeks. They die or go insane; Hector's widow and son are left in command. Troy has risen again.

All this allows the reader to construct an up-beat ending to the play. It cannot be a happy ending—there is too much bloodshed and suffering for that—but through all the disaster it allows us to see the victory of the good cause and the re-establishment of a moral order. In a similar way Sophocles's *Electra* or Shakespeare's *Macbeth* both end with the death of the unjust and the restoration of the rightful line. In such a view of the play Andromaque will be the positive heroine, and Hector the embodiment of justice.

But why should we consider Andromaque's cause preferable to that of the Greeks? It is partly because of the moral hierarchy mentioned earlier in this chapter; if Andromaque is understood as the embodiment of dignified suffering, to most readers she will seem more admirable than the representatives of the Greeks. Also, as the Magnificat suggests, there is satisfaction in the triumph of the humiliated and the downfall of the conquerors. Moreover, Andromaque has on her side two powerful figures, the child and the dead hero—Astyanax is all innocence and Hector radiates a god-like splendour. To Andromaque her husband is perfection itself; talking with Céphise at the end of Act III, she evokes a tragic but golden image of the warrior prince with his wife and child which recalls a memorable passage in Book 6 of the *Iliad*. Annotating the *Iliad* not long before he wrote *Andromaque*, Racine had described this scene as the 'entretien divin d'Hector et d'Andromaque', and had made a similar comment on Andromache's 'paroles divines' in her final farewell to Hector. The *Iliad* ends with the words: 'Such were the funeral rites of Hector, tamer of horses', and I think it is true to say that in modern times Hector has almost always been a nobler figure than the petulant Achilles—think for instance of Shakespeare's *Troilus and Cressida*. So the chances are that the reader will indeed associate Hector (and Troy) with justice.

Yet there is another image of Hector, an image fleetingly evoked in Oreste's ambassadorial speech of Act I:

> Ne vous souvient-il plus, Seigneur, quel fut Hector?
> Nos peuples affaiblis s'en souviennent encor.
> Son nom seul fait frémir nos veuves et nos filles. . . . (I.ii)

This is Hector, burner of ships, and, what is more, Oreste projects this incendiary image forward on to Astyanax:

> Et qui sait ce qu'un jour ce fils peut entreprendre?
> Peut-être dans nos ports nous le verrons descendre,
> Tel qu'on a vu son père embraser nos vaisseaux,
> Et, la flamme à la main, les suivre sur les eaux.

Or, more directly to Pyrrhus:

Vous-même de vos soins craignez la récompense,
Et que dans votre sein ce serpent élevé
Ne vous punisse un jour de l'avoir conservé.

Of course this is all the dubious rhetoric of the Greek envoy, and yet in a roundabout way he is right—it is Pyrrhus's protection of Astyanax that kills him, and Andromaque emerges at the end not as the suffering victim, but as the new conqueror. In this view Andromaque's victory is less a victory for justice than a continuation of the old feud and an example of the inflexible and disastrous power of the past over the present. Andromaque remains obstinately faithful to this past; even in the marriage ceremony of the final act she is described as blind and deaf to her present surroundings. Pyrrhus on the other hand seeks to make a new start. In answer to Oreste's demand that he complete his father's destructive work, he invokes the demands of life, trying to exorcize the image of burning Troy. Similarly, he strives to convince Andromaque of the need to forget what is past:

Peut-on haïr sans cesse? et punit-on toujours? (I.iv)

Like the love of Romeo for Juliet or that of Rodrigue for Chimène in Corneille's *Le Cid*, his love for Andromaque crosses the sacred barrier. He wants to do the impossible, to reconcile the irreconcilable.

He fails of course, just as Oedipus fails to escape from the past in which he had killed his father and married his mother. Coming from different sides, the demands of Hector and those of Hermione and the Greeks thwart his attempt to create a new life—the old feud takes its toll. One could say perhaps that Pyrrhus's sacrifice does after all allow the final resolution of the conflict; in the first version of the play (as published in 1668) Andromaque reappeared in the final act and declared that Pyrrhus's death had miraculously lessened Hector's hold on her:

Pyrrhus de mon Hector semble avoir pris la place.

But in Racine's final version this scene is omitted. Andromaque does not reappear, and the conclusion is one of bloodshed, madness and continuing war.

So we can read in *Andromaque* either the restoration of the just Trojan cause and the proper self-destruction of the Greeks, or else the terrible and meaningless aftermath of a meaningless war. Almost all tragic endings combine in this way elements of destruction and restoration. Heroes suffer and are killed, but some sort of order emerges. Where we lay the stress in *Andromaque* depends to a large extent on what we are looking for.

Andromaque *and Other Texts*

Both in this chapter and the previous one I have repeatedly referred to other books and plays which may influence and enrich one's reading of *Andromaque*. Like all his contemporaries, Racine sought not so much to invent new material as to present his own reworking of time-honoured themes, and with the exception of *Bajazet* all his tragedies tell old stories of heroes who occupy familiar places in the classical or biblical tradition. Obviously, then, it is as well for the reader to know something of this tradition. I would go further and say that much of the power and interest of Racine's play derives from the way it recalls the *Aeneid* and the *Iliad*, so that anyone reading it would do well to read or reread these classic texts. As well as Homer and Virgil, it also echoes many of the tragedies of antiquity and (for the more knowledgeable) such seventeenth-century French texts as Corneille's *Pertharite*.

It should not be thought that 'sources' are all that matter here. Works which Racine had not read may throw a great deal of light on *Andromaque*—for English readers Shakespearian tragedy is an inevitable and valuable point of reference. For a modern reading of the play, Baudelaire's poem *Le Cygne*, with its image of Andromache as the swan in exile on dry land, is arguably as important as any seventeenth-century tragedy that Racine may have known when he wrote his play. Or, to go outside the realm of texts, there is Jacques Rivette's haunting film *L'Amour Fou*, which is built round a rehearsal of *Andromaque*.

These are one or two hints from an immense range of possibilities. A short introduction is not the place to explore the endless relations between texts, but it does seem important to say a few words here about the place of *Andromaque* in the complete body of Racine's eleven tragedies. My aim here is not to trace the evolution of the playwright, but to see what patterns emerge when we place all these plays side by side. Such comparisons may give us some material with which to frame our own answer to the unanswerable question: what is Racinian tragedy? For most of Racine's contemporaries tragedy was a formal category, distinct from comedy, pastoral or tragi-comedy, but not implying any particular view of the world. By contrast modern theorists have put forward many accounts of the 'essence' of tragedy, and Racine's plays have been brought in line with most of these at one time or another. I do not wish to add to these attempts now, nor even to adjudicate between them, since their truth is hardly a matter for objective appraisal. Without, therefore, hoping to find a single unifying tragic vision, let us examine some of the constant features of Racine's tragedies—and these in turn may help to shape our reading of *Andromaque*.

Each of Racine's tragedies is different from the rest, but taken together they present a body of recurring situations and dramatic figures. These are combined in different ways, with different emphases, but there is no getting away from a fundamental sameness. To take the four principal characters first, although actors' interpretations may differ, we can still see in them representatives of important Racinian categories, categories which are by no means hard and fast divisions but which increase one's understanding of the isolated figures in a particular play. Thus Pyrrhus is one of the kings or emperors; all Racine's tragedies have a monarch as one of the main protagonists, and in almost every case the glorious monarch, usually a famous conqueror, is revealed as flawed, debased or tormented. The one exception is *Alexandre le Grand*, in which Racine openly flatters Louis XIV with the golden image of a ruler who is irresistible in love and war. Most often, and Pyrrhus is no exception, the monarch is torn between demands of state and private inclinations. More than this, Racine often brings home to his reader the contrast between the public stature of the king and his private degradation; there are many examples of this, from the psychopath Néron in *Britannicus* to the splendid yet treacherous Mithridate in the play that bears his name.

The other heroes of *Andromaque* can similarly be seen as members of the great Racinian families. Oreste is the doomed young man, echoed in a series of young male victims: his vacillating passivity brings him close to Antiochus in *Bérénice*, his violence and injustice to Pharnace in *Mithridate*. Hermione, the fierce young woman, resembles Eriphile in *Iphigénie*, and in some respects the passionate and self-tormenting Roxane (in *Bajazet*) and Phèdre or even, it might be argued, Bérénice. Andromaque, finally, is one of the virtuous victims who appear in almost all of Racine's plays, as indeed they do in subsequent melodrama. She is obviously different from any of Racine's other heroines in that she is a widow and a mother, but there is no mistaking the family resemblance that links her role to that of Junie, Iphigénie, Atalide, Monime, Aricie and Esther, all of them in some way dispossessed and captive, at the mercy of a powerful ruler.

These are the most important families, but other groupings may cut across them. Pyrrhus, for instance, also belongs to the group of the rebellious sons, who strive to throw off the burdens imposed by the past. In several of Racine's tragedies the son is shown at odds with the parent (Néron with Agrippine, Hippolyte with Thésée); in others no parent is present but forces from the past press down on the young man—the Trojan War and Hector in *Andromaque*, Rome and Vespasian in *Bérénice*, the absent sultan Amurat in *Bajazet*. On this quasi-Freudian reading we may want to set Pyrrhus alongside the young Xipharès rather than his father Mithridate; in both cases the young hero is in love with a forbidden woman.

Racine's dramatic figures are locked together in conflict, fighting to assert their power over one another. One of the principal sources of tension is unanswered love; *Andromaque* gives us the classic statement of this theme, which is echoed time and again in the other tragedies. What distinguishes this play from many of the others is that it does not contain a young couple whose mutual love is threatened by a more powerful figure (ruler or parent); this situation, fundamental to traditional comedy, is present in *La Thébaïde*, *Britannicus*, *Bérénice*, *Bajazet*, *Mithridate*, *Iphigénie* and *Phèdre*. These young lovers, often regarded by critics as rather insipid, provide a positive force which is set against the dark power of the monarchs and which in two cases actually overcomes them. The specific feature of *Andromaque* is that such mutual love exists only between Andromaque herself and two people who never appear, a young boy and a dead man. In this respect it is the most comfortless of Racine's plays.

As we have seen, the theme of reversal is all-pervading in *Andromaque*; blinded by desire, the protagonists pull down disaster on themselves. This pattern is vital in all Racine's tragedies, the main differentiation being between plays of general destruction and those in which the destruction of the 'wicked' or the powerful is counterbalanced by the victory of the oppressed or the 'good'. In the first group we should place *La Thébaïde*, *Britannicus*, *Bérénice*, *Bajazet* and *Phèdre*, in the second *Alexandre*, *Mithridate*, *Iphigénie*, *Esther* and *Athalie*. That *Andromaque* is midway between the two can be seen by comparing it with two plays that have unmistakably positive endings, *Iphigénie* and *Athalie*; and with both of these it has a great deal in common.

Iphigénie retells the old story of the sacrifice (or apparent sacrifice) of Agamemnon's daughter Iphigenia; this is needed to make the winds change and thus allow the Greek fleet to sail for Troy. It is interesting to set it alongside *Andromaque* in the first place because it looks at the Trojan War from the other end; where *Andromaque* is dominated by images from the violent past, *Iphigénie* looks forward enthusiastically to a triumphant war of conquest. In it moreover we see some of the Homeric heroes who are spoken of so admiringly by their children in *Andromaque*, and we see them (Agamemnon in particular) to be as powerless as other human beings. Like *Andromaque*, *Iphigénie* centres on a sacrifice and an altar; in both plays the Greek cause demands the killing of an innocent and in both plays the innocent is saved. In Racine's version of the Iphigenia story it is not the Greek princess who dies but her rival Eriphile, a character similar to Hermione in her unanswered love and in the jealous fury with which she sets in motion a train of events leading to her own death at the altar. So the 'wicked' heroine is hoist with her own petard—but she is the only one to suffer. Apart from the virtuous Iphigénie all the other characters are vacillating, violent or unscrupulous, but they are saved from self-destruction by the death of the scapegoat, and the play ends on a note of rejoicing at what looks like divine intervention. By contrast the 'up-beat' element in the ending of *Andromaque* is overshadowed by the general collapse. If we did not know that it was written several years earlier we might have imagined that it was a bitter rejection of the providential and heroic optimism which triumphs against all the odds in *Iphigénie*.

The story of *Athalie* comes not from Greek legend, but from the Old Testament. It tells of the killing of the usurper Athaliah and the restoration of the line of David in the person of the boy-king Joas. Although *Athalie* has none of the destructive love between the sexes which so fills *Andromaque*, the two plays are alike in that in both an unexpected turn of events humbles those who enjoy all the power at the outset and raises up the apparently helpless victims. The defencelessness of Astyanax and Joas is described in similar terms and set against the fury of the oppressor. Where Pyrrhus was the butcher of Priam and Polyxenes, Athalie had massacred her own grandchildren; she, like Pyrrhus, is surrounded with the language of blood and violence. Both monarchs are tempted to go against their *raison d'état* and befriend the boys who eventually take their place. Just as Oreste warns Pyrrhus against sheltering Astyanax, Mathan the high priest tells Athalie:

> Quelque monstre naissant dans ce temple s'élève,
> Reine. N'attendez pas que le nuage crève. (II.vi)

And in both plays the monarch, deceived by a trick (Andromaque's 'innocent stratagème'), is led to the altar and killed, whereupon the young king and his protagonists assume power—execution and coronation. The difference of course is that in *Athalie* the killing is done by the supporters of Joas; the ending is the culmination of a well-laid plot, rather than the result of a series of clashes and misunderstandings. Moreover, the restoration of Joas is hailed as the work of the all-powerful and true god, to whom a chorus sings throughout the play. Even so, the triumphant quality of the conclusion is attenuated both by a vision of the future in which Joas will degenerate into a tyrant and by the admiration and sympathy which Athalie tends to win from many readers or spectators. In her eyes the god of the Jews is as cruel as the malicious gods accused by Oreste.

   Athalie and *Andromaque* follow one of the most basic and ancient tragic patterns, the death of the king; both plays allow one to conclude, with differing degrees of enthusiasm: 'the King is dead, long live the King.' *Athalie* goes further, and explicitly connects the restoration of Joas with the coming of Christ. Is it possible that something of the kind is present allegorically in *Andromaque*, that the figures of mother and child and the final combination of death and renewal carry Christian overtones? Perhaps—though it is also possible that the memory of plays such as *Andromaque* will encourage a non-Christian reading of *Athalie*. These are matters for the individual reader; as for what *Andromaque* may have meant for Racine and his contemporaries, that is the subject of the following chapter.

4. Racine and his Time

   So far we have explored ways in which *Andromaque* can be performed, read, enjoyed or understood by people today. Not surprisingly, however, this has involved frequent glances at previous readings and performances. We do not live entirely in the present. We may not want to be historians, but we can hardly help looking back for help in interpreting things that survive from the past. Indeed, if we should find Racine's play an alien experience and his meanings uncongenial, the historical approach may be the only one open to us. And even if this is not the case, and we feel some continuity from Racine to the present time, it still seems to me that one of the values of reading books or seeing plays written long ago must be that it encourages us to go outside our present surroundings and understand historically something that was not written for us.

   The questions I have been asking in the first two chapters are open ones. It may take experience to make the most of *Andromaque*, but in the end the proof of the pudding is in the eating; a good production is one that works, a good critical reading is one that stimulates and satisfies. Now, however, we are concerned with historical questions, and external evidence is needed. What is more, the evidence is potentially inexhaustible, ranging from minute points of Racine's biography to overall views of the structure and evolution of French society in the seventeenth century. At best, as in all history, we can only look for plausible hypotheses.

Racine and Literature

Let us look first at the person who produced the text. We do not know Racine's life in nearly as much detail as we should have for a modern writer, but here is a framework of biography for *Andromaque*. Jean Racine was born in 1639 in a provincial bourgeois family; left an orphan, he was brought up by his grandmother and then at schools run by the Jansenists, a puritanical and much-persecuted Catholic sect. He appears to have become estranged from the Jansenists fairly soon after leaving school and broke openly with them in 1666 by publishing a caustic pamphlet against their condemnation of the theatre. Only after 1677 was he reconciled with them. In 1660 he published his first literary work, an ode on the wedding of Louis XIV; after an unsuccessful attempt to enter the Church, he made a career in literature, receiving an official pension and gradually rising in society to become a favourite of the King. *Andromaque*, produced at the end of 1667 and published in 1668, was his third play to be performed. It was preceded by *La Thébaïde* (1664) and *Alexandre le Grand* (1665). Both of these were performed by Molière's company of actors, but Racine quickly transferred the successful *Alexandre* to the more highly reputed Hôtel de Bourgogne theatre, who were to perform the rest of his secular plays. At the time of the composition of *Andromaque*, Racine was apparently in love with Thérèse Du Parc, an actress from Molière's theatre who also went over to the Hôtel de Bourgogne.

This is only an outline, but for the period around 1667 we do not have much other direct information. There are for instance no letters talking about the play. At most, there are the two prefaces (of 1668 and 1676), which Racine wrote *after* the play, mainly in order to answer criticism. What these two pieces suggest above all—and the same is true of most of Racine's utterances on the theatre—is that he was preoccupied with specifically *literary* problems, and in particular the relation of his play to other books. For this one play he refers to Virgil's *Aeneid*, Euripides's *Andromache*, Seneca's *Troades*, D'Urfé's *Astrée*, Horace's *Ars Poetica*, Aristotle's *Poetics*, Ronsard's *Franciade*, Euripides's *Helen* and a commentary on Sophocles's *Electra*. This suggests that if we want to understand the production of *Andromaque* we should look in the first place to Racine's previous contacts with literature, his reading, his comments, his own writing.

For the period from 1660 to 1663, unlike the period of the great tragedies, we have quite a lot of Racine's letters. These show that he shared with other literary people of his time a powerful and well-informed interest in questions of poetic language and a wide range of reading in Latin, Italian, Spanish and French. Not surprisingly Virgil, who is to be so important for *Andromaque*, is repeatedly mentioned or quoted. What is exceptional, however, though it is not so evident in these letters, is Racine's appreciation of Greek literature. We know that his education with the Jansenists of Port-Royal had given him a far greater knowledge of Greek than most of his educated contemporaries, his annotations of many Greek classics have survived, and it is surely no accident that he chose so many Greek subjects for his own plays. Later in his career he was to single out Euripides as his great model and in the preface to *Iphigénie* (1674) he gave his adversaries a lesson in the correct reading of the ancients. He and his friend the poet Boileau came to be known as 'Messieurs du Sublime' for their championing of noble antiquity against what they saw as a more frivolous modernity.

At the time of *Andromaque* it is not quite so clear where Racine stands. The early letters show him quite happy with the elegant games of the fashionable poet, playing with words and taking pleasure in what he calls 'le creux'. They also contain some mockery of the old-fashioned taste of an older generation, and it is this that comes to the fore both in Racine's anti-Jansenist pamphlet of 1666 and in several of his prefaces. In the preface to *Andromaque* he tries to distinguish Pyrrhus from the 'Céladons', the heroes of the old novels, but most frequently his aim in the prefaces is to define his own sort of tragedy in opposition to that represented by the ageing Pierre Corneille. Corneille was still regarded by many as king of the Paris stage, and the ambitious Racine was eager to seize his crown. The clearest statement of this comes in the preface to *Britannicus* (1670), where he says that in order to satisfy his critics

Au lieu d'une action simple, chargée de peu de matière, telle que doit être une action qui se passe en un seul jour, et qui s'avançant par degrés vers sa fin, n'est soutenue que par les intérêts, les sentiments et les passions des personnages, il faudrait remplir cette même action de quantité d'incidents qui ne se pourrait passer qu'en un mois, d'un grand nombre de jeux de théâtre, d'autant plus surprenants qu'ils seraient moins vraisemblables, d'une infinité de déclamations où l'on ferait dire aux acteurs tout le contraire de ce qu'il devraient dire.

And he goes on to give mocking examples from Corneille's plays of the 1660s. This suggests that his aim was to produce a new kind of simple, believable and moving tragedy, modelled on the Greeks and avoiding the elaborate plots and extravagant eloquence of his rivals. Not that Racine ever rejects the basic norms of French classical tragedy, with its small number of noble characters, its verse, its unities of time, place and action and its use of the five-act pattern to maintain and increase excitement. He is concerned rather to stake out his territory within this area.

Very schematically then, one can see a number of formal influences at work on Racine as he wrote *Andromaque*—the general conventions governing all French classical tragedy, the rejection of some particular versions of this tradition such as that embodied in Pierre Corneille's plays, the model of passionate simplicity found in Greek tragedy, and the memories of the *Aeneid*, the *Iliad* and many other sources. A good account of the sources will be found in Jean Pommier's *Tradition littéraire et modèles vivants dans l'Andromaque de Racine*. Without wishing to belittle the importance of these reminiscences of earlier literature, I would, however, agree with Michael Edwards (in *La Tragédie racinienne*, p. 102) that the most interesting of all the literary antecedents of *Andromaque* are in fact Racine's two preceding plays. *La Thébaïde ou les Frères Ennemis* takes what Racine calls 'le sujet le plus tragique de l'antiquité', the story of the mutual killing of the warring twin sons of Oedipus. Whereas Corneille in his reworking of the Oedipus story (*Oedipe*, 1660) had attenuated the horror of the original, Racine presses his to the extreme, killing off all the main characters and presenting the spectator with a vision of irremediable discord in which even the innocent are doomed and the best intentions produce catastrophic effects. The play stresses that what divides the brothers is not so much ambition (which was normal in tragedy of the time) as an inborn pre-natal enmity. Like Oreste, Jocaste, the mother of the heroes, sees the whole situation as evidence of the heavens' malevolence. Even Créon, who is usually seen as a level-headed politician, is here a love-crazed villain who finally succumbs to a fatal frenzy reminiscent of the 'fureurs' of Oreste. The play is written in a vehement style with powerful clashes of eloquence.

Alexandre le Grand, which tells of one of Alexander's conquests, is quite different. It too has its oratorical duels, but generally the language is more varied and more elegant. Where hate and ambition had dominated *La Thébaide*, here love comes to the fore. Although the play shows us rivalries between the main characters and in particular the triumph of Alexandre's 'generosity' over the defeated but magnanimous prince Porus, the heroes' actions are in fact intended above all to please the women they love. There is one unloved Oreste-like individual, whose death casts a shadow over the ending, but the other main characters show a perfect combination of love and magnanimity so that the play can end in political reconciliation and the prospect of a double wedding. Pyrrhus may or may not reflect the old novels, but Alexandre, Porus, Cléofile and Axiane certainly do. *Alexandre* presents a golden image of amorous heroism.

Never again did Racine return to the extreme horrors of *La Thébaide* or the rather hollow glory of its successor. *Andromaque*, like many of Racine's later plays, brings together elements from these two early tragedies, the dream of heroic possibilities with the nightmare of human degradation and irreconcilable conflict. And above all, destructive discord is here shown as springing from the love which *Alexandre* had shown in such an admirable light. How far Racine was conscious of *Andromaque* as a continuation or a synthesis of his previous plays we cannot tell, but there is no doubt that a reading of them helps one to understand something about the genesis of the later work.

Finally, in talking about the composition of *Andromaque*, one must remember that the play as we usually see or read it is the product of a number of changes. We have no manuscript to trace all the early changes that preceded the first publication, but the published version of 1668 was subsequently revised more than once before reaching its final form. These variants can be found in many modern editions of the play. A lot of them are of only minor interest, but there is one crucial one: in Act V, Scene iii of the original version of Andromaque is brought on (as a hostage) by Oreste, she pronounces a longish speech declaring her new allegiance to Pyrrhus and is then released by Hermione, since 'Pyrrhus ainsi l'ordonne.' One imagines that Racine wanted to bring back his heroine, who otherwise does not appear after Act IV, Scene i, and as we have seen in the last chapter, this original ending produces a rather different emphasis. The final version is certainly more concentrated, and probably more satisfying dramatically, but if one wants to understand the play as it was in 1667 one must go back to the first text.

The Literary Context

The preceding pages have dealt with Racine's own literary concerns and what can be deduced about his intentions in composing *Andromaque*. Now we must widen the scope of the enquiry and see the play not so much from the point of view of the author as from that of the public. Who composed this public and what were the literary habits and expectations which conditioned their reception of Racine's tragedy? In other words, what is the place of *Andromaque* in the literary world of its time?

Racine was not writing for most of the twenty million people of France. Many so-called French people did not actually speak French, and among those who did only a minority could read. A very much smaller minority had the leisure and the money to go to theatres or read books. Paris, a city of half a million inhabitants, had much the greatest proportion of readers and theatregoers, but even here it seems that only about 15,000 people went to see successful plays. The cheapest theatre places were beyond the means of most people, books were a luxury commodity, and lending libraries were virtually non-existent.

In part, *Andromaque* was written for the pleasure of the most exalted group of all, the royal court. It was first performed on 17 November 1667 in the Queen's apartments before the King and Queen and 'quantité de seigneurs et de dames de la cour'. Moreover, as the dedication proudly tells us, Racine had given readings of his play to the King's sister-in-law, Henriette d'Angleterre, who had apparently given him advice and help in composing it. Naturally, however, Racine's real theatre public was wider than this select gathering. Performed at the Hôtel de Bourgogne theatre, his play had a great success, comparable to that achieved by Corneille's *Le Cid* thirty years earlier. Here too there were many noble spectators, but the audience included also many of the richer or more educated members of the third estate (lawyers, merchants, etc.). Here too were those who made a living by some sort of writing; many of these, like Racine, were bourgeois in origin.

Our knowledge of theatre audiences is not as precise as it might be, but we know even less about the people who read *Andromaque*. Racine was naturally a closed book to the peasants who made up the overwhelming majority of the population. Even among the better-off, however, not everyone bought books; those who did were more likely to possess works on religion than the frivolous productions of modern literature. On the other hand, Racine's plays were being used before long in the rhetoric classes of the schools—they had become classics. In any case, we shall not go far wrong in thinking of *Andromaque* as addressed to a small, privileged group whose members shared many of the same values and tastes.

As far as language is concerned, Racine's play conforms to many of the habits of this group. To start with an obvious point, it reflects a state of the language which is not the same as modern French; we should remember that there have been changes in pronunciation (for instance, seventeenth-century actors would not have pronounced the final consonant in 'Pyrrhus') in syntax, and in the meaning of words. When Pyrrhus says to *Andromaque*: 'Ah! que vous me gênez!' (I.iv), the verb has a meaning closer to its etymological sense of 'to torture' than in modern French. Important words such as 'gloire', 'transport' or 'maîtresse' all need to be looked up in a historical dictionary, and even words which apparently mean more or less the same now as in 1667 are likely to carry different connotations in the context of seventeenth-century literature. This means that the more one reads of the writing of Racine's contemporaries, the nearer one will come to 'knowing' their language—though at best this 'knowing' is only an act of imagination.

As has often been remarked, the language of Racine's tragedies reflects a culture of exclusion, or at least of strict hierarchy in which tragedy demands a language quite different from that of satire. The people in *Andromaque* do not talk like ordinary people, their language excludes almost all 'low' words, provincial words, technical words, words evoking everyday physical existence, work, food and so on. Many ordinary words are replaced by their poetic substitutes—'mariage' by 'hymen', 'colère' by 'courroux', 'amour' by 'flamme'. In all this *Andromaque* conforms with the norms of contemporary literary language. However, within this narrow field, Racine's audiences were interested in the stylistic choices made by writers. The male members of the public had mostly had a thorough training in rhetoric, language was an important subject of conversation in the *salons*, and criticism of literature was largely concerned with questions of style and language. There is much in *Andromaque* to satisfy those with a taste for formal eloquence. As we saw in the first chapter, even passionate speeches are generally well made, and there are certain passages which go much further in the direction of the rhetoric of display; the most obvious example is the pair of speeches made in Act I, Scene ii by Oreste and Pyrrhus, beautifully formed tirades using all the resources of eloquence both in the marshalling of arguments and the evocative use of language.

> Je songe quelle était autrefois cette ville
> Si superbe en remparts, en héros si fertile,
> Maîtresse de l'Asie; et je regarde enfin
> Quel fut le sort de Troie et quel est son destin.
> Je ne vois que des tours que la cendre a couvertes,
> Un fleuve teint de sang, des campagnes désertes,
> Un enfant dans les fers; et je ne puis songer
> Que Troie en cet état aspire à se venger. (I.iv)

This is the language of the orator. Another form of fine speaking which appealed to many contemporaries was the extravagance of the *précieux* lover, as we see it for instance in the metaphors and paradoxes of Oreste:

> Madame, c'est à vous de prendre une victime
> Que les Scythes auraient dérobée à vos coups,
> Si j'en avais trouvé d'aussi cruels que vous. (II.ii)

However, as I suggested earlier, speeches such as these almost invariably have a clear dramatic function in *Andromaque*, being contrasted with quite different ways of speaking. Racine does not deny his public the varied pleasures of fine language, but he generally subordinates this to the demands of economy and 'naturalness'. A taste for a less glittering, more sober style seems to have been fashionable in the 1660s; a number of the younger writers, critics and rhetoricians were contemptuous of old-fashioned 'galimatias' or over-elaborate language, and it seems likely that some of the public were on their side even if others regretted the grand eloquence (or grandiloquence) of an earlier generation. For it is very much a question of generations. I showed in the first chapter how Racine's language marks a step on the road towards 'life-like' dialogue as compared with that of *Horace*. By the 1660s all writers of tragedy, including Pierre Corneille, were writing in a less overtly oratorical manner, but if one compares *Andromaque* to plays by such contemporaries as Thomas Corneille and Philippe Quinault, one is constantly struck by the relative energy and directness of Racine's writing. None of his contemporaries were normally capable of the eloquent simplicity of lines such as Hermione's

> Ah! je ne croyais pas qu'il fût si près d'ici (II.i)

or Andromaque's

>   Oui, je m'y trouverai. Mais allons voir mon fils. (IV.i)

Beyond these questions of language and style, what can we discover
about the relation of *Andromaque* to the literature of the time? I have
already said something about Racine's probable sources; now it is a
question of seeing the play as a contemporary might have seen it, one
among many contemporary writings. The literary field is an immense
one, since for a given public it included not only what was being written
in one particular year, but all that continued to be read; for the public of
1667 this may have meant such things as the Latin classics, the early
tragedies of Corneille, and the long novels written ten, twenty or even
fifty years earlier. It also included many different genres from court
poetry to religious polemic. But this is not the place for a grand literary
tableau, and I shall confine myself to the immediately relevant areas of
tragedy, tragi-comedy and the novel.

As far as 'serious' theatre is concerned, various different tendencies vied
for public favour. One of the most popular—and one very different from
Andromaque—seems to have been the *pièce à machines*, the spectacular
show with all sorts of brilliant stage effects, music, dancing and so on. The
Marais theatre mounted one of these most seasons; it is probable that in
the 1667–8 season they were continuing to perform the success of the
previous year, Boyer's *Les Amours de Jupiter et de Semele*. It is interesting
that Boyer had chosen a subject from Greek antiquity; similarly Pierre
Corneille's two machine plays dramatize the stories of Andromeda and
the Golden Fleece, and later, when opera came into fashion, some of
Quinault's first libretti had Greek subjects. By contrast, 'straight' tragedy
was more often set in a rather nebulous Asia or in some corner of the
Roman empire; Racine was unusual in choosing one of the central Greek
legends for a serious play. Boyer's *Jupiter et Semele* is in fact called a
tragedy because it ends in the death of Semele and her human lover and it
contains a prologue in which Boyer defends tragedy against what he
describes as the contemporary taste for comedy. In his *Critique de l'Ecole
des Femmes* (1663), Molière had claimed that tragedy was easy to write
because it called simply for heroic exaggeration and idealization, whereas
comedy depended on truthful representation. Boyer, rather than
asserting that tragedy also is truthful, defends it for its uplifting qualities,
since it shows us 'la gloire des héros et la vertu romaine'.

Boyer's phase is perhaps an indication of what many of Racine's
contemporaries expected of tragedy. Pierre Corneille was the accredited

purveyor of heroic sentiments, although in fact many of his late tragedies involve complicated and sordid matrimonial bargaining rather than the clash of great wills. His latest play at the time of *Andromaque* was *Attila*, performed by Molière's company with considerable success in the spring of 1667. It gives a good idea of the 'Cornelian' style of tragedy which was also written by Corneille's younger brother Thomas and other contemporaries. The interest is centred on the intrigues surrounding Attila, the scourge of God, and the fundamental concern of the play is a struggle for power in which various individuals display their force of character as they are faced by terrible dilemmas. The hero is not a virtuous figure, but he is larger than life in his cruel strength of purpose; the other main characters are all noble in their sentiments, though as usual in late Corneille the women are more forceful than the men. The atmosphere of sinister plotting may well strike a modern reader as grotesque, particularly when Attila dies of a bleeding nose and the virtuous triumph, but it gave contemporary audiences a feast of what Boyer called 'nobles mouvements, belles passions, grands sentiments'.

In *Attila* and comparable power tragedies the heroes and heroines are often portrayed as in love, but generally love is a means rather than an end. There was, however, a sort of play in which love was the prime mover: the tragedy or tragi-comedy which kept alive the major theme of the long novels of Mademoiselle de Scudéry, where great heroes of antiquity are shown to be impelled not so much by patriotism, ambition or honour as by their devoted love for their ladies. In 1665 Boileau had written (but not published) a satirical dialogue (*Les Héros de roman*) mocking this fashion and singling out Philippe Quinault's *Astrate* as the prime example of its dramatic variant. Boileau's hostility did not prevent *Astrate*, first performed in 1664, from enjoying a great success, presumably because of its idealizing portrayal of love. Like *Attila*, it involves a power struggle, but now the centre of the stage is occupied by two perfect lovers, Astrate the prince and Elise the usurping queen. As in the standard tragi-comedy a false identity provides an agonizing problem for the lovers, but, unlike a tragi-comedy, Quinault's play ends tragically with the death of the prince and the queen. However, the dominant impression is one of perfect if rather verbose love—as Boileau put it in one of his satires, 'et jusqu'à "Je vous hais", tout se dit tendrement.'

Such, briefly sketched, is the immediate context of *Andromaque*. In many ways of course, Racine's tragedy meets the expectations of all theatregoers of the time: it has the familiar noble characters, five-act

structure and verse form. As we saw earlier, Racine declared himself in
favour of a simpler plot than those found in many contemporary
tragedies. *Andromaque* is by no means his simplest play, but it is a good
deal less involved than many plays of the time, and it is completely
devoid of such devices as disguise, mistaken identities or oracles, and has
nothing to do with the spectacular supernatuiral of the machine plays. In
all of this Racine is the proponent of a fashionable tendency and he also
moves with the times in replacing political power by love as the moving
force of his play. Indeed this was sufficient for many contemporaries to
see him as working in the same vein as Quinault—for such spectators he
was 'le tendre Racine'. Nor did many people apparently see any major
difference between *Andromaque* and *Alexandre*, whereas today it seems
obvious that *Alexandre*, like *Astrate*, portrays heroic sentiments and
perfect love, and *Andromaque* does neither. Grandeur is not absent from
the later play, but Boyer's 'nobles mouvements, belles passions, grands
sentiments' are set against a much less glamorous image of humanity.
Similarly the ending of Racine's play is more catastrophic than those of
Attila and *Astrate*. Attila dies, but he is a monster and his death clears the
way for general happiness; Astrate and Elise die, but in a sort of *Liebestod*,
crushed by circumstance, but still heroic and beautiful. *Andromaque*, by
contrast, whatever one may think of the 'resurrection of Troy',
recaptures some of the feeling of radical disaster that one finds in many
Greek tragedies. In this, as in his use of central Greek sources, Racine is an
exception among playwrights of his time.

   This is not to say, however, that Racine was on his own. What Paul
Bénichou, in his *Morales du Grand Siècle*, has called the 'demolition of the
hero' was as important a tendency in the writing of the 1660s as the
reaction against flamboyant language. Perhaps it did not represent the
taste of the majority, but those writers of the period who are still read all
tell a similar tale: Pascal, La Rochefoucauld, Boileau, Molière, even
Corneille in many of his later tragedies, cast a mocking or pessimistic
light on the heroic imagery of the time. Perhaps this can be seen most
clearly of all in the fiction of Madame de Lafayette, not only the famous
La Princesse de Clèves, but even the short story *La Princesse de Montpensier*,
published as early as 1662. This is a love story, full of deception,
ingratitude, infidelity and suffering; great men and women from French
history are seen in their *misère* as well as their *grandeur* and just as
Andromaque is set against the legendary backcloth of the Trojan War, the
love intrigues of *La Princesse de Montpensier* are interwoven with the wars
of religion and the bloody massacre of St Bartholomew. Readers who

had responded to this story were well prepared to appreciate Racine's tragedy.

Literature and Life

With a certain amount of reading it is not difficult to see the place occupied by *Andromaque* in the literary life of its day. Should one perhaps go further and say with Jean Giraudoux that a literary approach to Racine's tragedies is the only fruitful one, since 'il n'est pas un sentiment en Racine qui ne soit un sentiment littéraire' (*Littérature*, Gallimard, p. 22)? Or, on the contrary, can we not do something with the common-sense assumption that books are produced not only in answer to other books, but in answer to the needs and desires of an author and his readers? What was Racine expressing of his own experience and inner life? And what could *Andromaque* appeal to in the life and aspirations of contemporary society?

Andromaque is a far cry from an autobiographical novel, but it is possible to glimpse in it what appear to be direct reflections of Racine's own life. One can for instance quote passages from his personal writings and show how they are borne out by the play. Thus the letters written in 1662 from the southern town of Uzès reveal Racine as an observer of local conflict: 'Ils ne travaillent à autre chose qu'à se tuer tous tant qu'ils sont'; and of the force of passion, 'En ce pays-ci on ne voit guère d'amours médiocres; toutes les passions y sont démesurées.' How like *Andromaque*, we may think! More to the point, we see Racine learning to play the game of intrigue and dissimulate his real feelings as so many of his characters are obliged to do. Other letters show him as ambitious, selfish and capable of callous ingratitude. The Jansenist schools of Port-Royal had been a second home to the orphan Racine; whether he was happy there we cannot tell, but at the very least he was indebted to his masters for an exceptional education and a number of useful connections. But in 1666, when he was perhaps planning *Andromaque*, he held the Jansenists up to ridicule in his *Lettre à l'auteur des Hérésies Imaginaires*, telling humiliating stories against them and exposing the vanity of their literary pretensions. By composing *Andromaque* he was compounding the offence to those who saw writers of novels and plays as *empoisonneurs publics*, corrupting audiences with their vivid depiction of human passion. Finally, at about the same time, we see Racine betraying the trust of Molière, who had given him his start in the theatre.

In view of all this, it is perhaps natural to ask whether there is not a personal explanation for the emphasis given to ingratitude and betrayal in *Andromaque*. Both Pyrrhus and Oreste betray their trust, and Pyrrhus in particular is portrayed as tormented by the burden of obligation. Is it not probable that Racine is here giving expression to his feelings of frustration and self-reproach, and that in the person of Andromaque he represents an ideal of fidelity which he is conscious of betraying? A contemporary said of *Alexandre* what has often been said about novelists and dramatists 'On le [Racine] voyait dépeint dans chaque personnage.' The same is no doubt equally true—or untrue—of *Andromaque*.

Similarly, in a book entitled *Vers le vrai Racine*, René Jasinksi has tried to show that the love relationships in the play should be seen as a transposition of Racine's own situation. Pyrrhus is Racine and Andromaque the actress Thérèse Du Parc, who was also a widow as well as being the first person to play the part. Hermione is another (unidentified) woman, Oreste Racine on another occasion, and so on . . . This is all possible, but the enterprise strikes me as pointless and absurd. Racine may indeed have painted himself in all his characters, but the self in question does not have to be the self of actual lived experience. Since we know so little about the experience, all we can do is express a general opinion about the probable relation between people in books and people in life. 'Ecrit-on de tels vers sans une part d'aveu?' asks Jasinski of a piece of amorous eloquence. The honest answer has to be that we do not know.

Rather than a representation of Racine's own life, we may expect to find in *Andromaque* a representation of contemporary society. The critic Saint-Evremond complained that Racine's tragedies did indeed present seventeenth-century Frenchmen in ancient garb, and Racine constantly attempted in his prefaces to counter such attacks with claims of historical accuracy. Even so, situations involving princely or other arranged marriages and the resulting conflicts of obligation and inclination were familiar enough to contemporary audiences, and there is every reason to suppose that many of them saw a fairly idealized reflection of contemporary situations and characters in *Andromaque*. Most people at this time did not suppose that they were fundamentally very different from the ancient Greeks; although there were surface variations, they assumed that writers of all periods would represent 'human nature', so that the true representation of Homeric heroes would be equally valid for themselves, or for the centuries to come. So some years later Racine concluded from the success of *Iphigénie* that 'le bon sens et la raison étaient les mêmes dans tous les siècles.'

A book published two or three years before *Andromaque*, Bussy-Rabutin's *Histoire Amoureuse des Gaules*, gives the reader thinly disguised descriptions of contemporary amorous behaviour which often remind one of Racine's tragedy—stories of passion, ingratitude, blackmail and treachery, though presented in a comic and cycnical light. Bussy's 'Gauls' are in fact known individuals, just as Mademoiselle de Scudéry's novels had presented portraits of antique heroes which her readers applied immediately to particular contemporaries. The habit of reading with 'keys' of this sort was common in Racine's day and Racine himself almost certainly meant contemporaries to see Louis XIV and Condé in the heroes of *Alexandre*. But if he had such intentions in *Andromaque*, we no longer know them. At most there is the hint that the noble Andromaque is a flattering portrait of Henrietta Maria, the mother of Racine's protector Henriette d'Angleterre. Otherwise we must be content to point to the general reflection of contemporary manners in the play. Whether spectators found this reflection flattering, insulting or truthful it is hard to say, though posterity has made a lot of La Bruyère's curious remark to the effect that Corneille paints people as they should be, but Racine paints them as they really are.

It is not only in this sort of mirroring that a play such as *Andromaque* can be seen as related to Racine and his society. There are more indirect approaches—language for instance. I have already stressed the appropriateness of Racine's dramatic language to a restricted audience, but one might also expect to find in his style some reflection of his true nature (on the assumption that style is the man). This would necessarily involve reading and re-reading Racine's other plays until one could identify his 'voice', as one eventually comes to recognize the presence of Flaubert or Proust in their sentences. I think this is possible, in spite of Racine's much greater impersonality; a line such as 'Captive, toujours triste, importune à moi-même' does come to seem typically Racinian, but it remains very hard to show convincingly what particular elements of rhythm, syntax or vocabulary contribute to this individuality. And in any case this all remains strictly internal to the plays and does not tell us anything about their genesis. Its main virtue is that it makes us see one play as part of larger whole, on the basis of which we can create for ourselves an imagined author. But there is no ascertainable connection between this imagined author and the historical Jean Racine who was born in La Ferté-Milon in 1639. In this respect the author is *in* his writings, not behind them.

One comes a little nearer to the historical Racine with the

'psychocritical' approach adopted by Charles Mauron in his *L'Inconscient dans l'œuvre et la vie de Racine*. Mauron's book does in fact contain an interesting and often persuasive reading of *Andromaque*, stressing the central position of Pyrrhus. The real structure of the play only emerges, however, when it is seen alongside all the other plays; from the total body of tragedies Mauron isolates a configuration of relations which he sees as revealing Racine's unconscious obsessions. In Freudian terms, the 'ego', represented in *Andromaque* by Pyrrhus, is seen as subjugated by a dominating mother-figure (the forces of the past, Hermione, Andromaque's fidelity to the dead Hector), and trying vainly and guiltily to escape from this deathly fixation towards life (love of Andromaque, Astyanax). This fundamental structure is shown as evolving throughout Racine's writing career, and in the second part of his book Mauron looks for possible biographical explanations for it. Naturally enough he emphasizes Racine's position as an orphan brought up by women and then by the Jansenists of Port-Royal; the religion of Port-Royal is presented as neurotic and life-denying, and Mauron suggests that Racine's attempt to repress or sublimate this Jansenist 'fixation' is shown above all in the choice of writing as a career. All this finds an indirect expression in plays such as *Andromaque*, just as our unconscious drives issue forth in the disguised form of our dreams.

Mauron's Freudianism will not be accepted by everyone, but I am inclined to think that his book contributes an important element to any attempt to reconstruct the complex process that must have gone into the writing of *Andromaque*. Given the shortage of biographical data it is bound to be speculative, but so too is the apparently more empirical study of literary sources. Racine is so remote from us that any attempt to explain the genesis of *Andromaque* must remain highly tentative.

As well as these psychological tensions, which are probably as prevalent in many other societies as in that of seventeenth-century France, it seems likely that *Andromaque* also embodies attitudes and values which are specific to Racine's own age, attitudes and values which he shared with various contemporary social groups. As we saw in the last chapter, there is plenty of room for argument about the value system of the play, so we must not expect to find in it a clear expression of the values of one particular social group, but rather a meeting place of different and perhaps contradictory socio-political, moral and religious attitudes. Above all it must be remembered that we are not discussing the deliberate expression of such attitudes, but the unrealized assumptions that the play appeals to or is founded on.

In the first place the 'demolition of the hero', which can be seen in *Andromaque* and other writings of the time, coincides with a reduction of the power of the French nobility; as is well known, Louis XIV wanted to be master in his own kingdom and attempted to reduce the independence of the unruly princes and nobles. Racine's play is not part of a campaign, but it certainly seems to be in harmony with this historical movement. The heroic ethic of glamorous self-projection had suited the aspirations or delusions of the nobility, but this glory had been considerably tarnished, for instance, by the disasters of the Fronde, the civil war of 1648–53; compare the reductions of Pyrrhus's glory by the bloody descriptions of his Trojan exploits and by his unchivalrous behaviour towards Andromaque and Hermione.

As we have seen, Racine is unusual among serious dramatists of the time in giving such a disenchanted picture of noble humanity, but one may perhaps see in this lucid pessimism one manifestation of the new reason of an age in which it was easier to see through the illusions of human grandeur. Racine's France was very far from being a society founded on reason, but even so this was the age when the scientific revolution was beginning to take shape, the age which finally abandoned witchcraft trials. It has been argued that this new critical spirit is an expression of the values of the social group from which Racine himself came, a group that was gradually gaining a greater influence on the life of the nation, the bourgeoisie. One may agree that in the long run the decline of such values as ostentation, generosity, bravery and respect for noble birth made room for a more utilitarian value system which served the interests of the commercial bourgeoisie. However, nothing of this 'positive' vision is to be seen in *Andromaque*. In writing for his essentially aristocratic audience, Racine may have been undermining some of the illusions of their class or indeed echoing their taste for a more cynical self-awareness; similarly the noblemen Bussy-Rabutin and La Rochefoucauld seem to have taken pleasure in showing the base motives and ignoble passions of their peers. But I should say that in all these cases, even that of Bussy, the criticism does not lead to an alternative set of values (those of Racine's down-to-earth confidants perhaps), but to the reassertion of an old and perhaps impossible ideal. The people in Racine's play do not live up to the noble ideal, but there is little doubt that they ought to—the old values of generosity, sacrifice, fidelity, bravery seem to me to emerge unscathed.

Racine was of course writing in a Christian society, and had himself come under the powerful influence of Jansenist teachers. (Indeed he actually held an ecclesiastical benefice for some years, though this tells us nothing about his beliefs.) It seems natural then to see in the anti-heroic element of *Andromaque* not only a critique of the nobility, but a more general Christian (or Jansenist) condemnation of what contemporaries would have called *le monde*, the unredeemed and wicked world. Seventeenth-century France saw a vigorous revival of monastic orders, and the literature of the time makes a great deal of the contrast between life in the world, full of excitement and spiritual danger, and the holy retreat to *le désert*. Madame de Lafayette's *La Princesse de Clèves* is an excellent example. Bearing this in mind, we may well see in the doings of the Greeks an image of the damned (later to be brought up to date with Sartre's 'L'enfer c'est les autres'), and in Oreste's final vision a glimpse of Hell. Andromaque, by contrast, in her renunciation of the world ('Seigneur, tant de grandeurs ne nous touchent plus guère'), echoes the resignation of the nun.

A particular version of this rejection of the world is described in Lucien Goldmann's book, *Le Dieu Caché*, a study of the tragic world-view of the Jansenists. Giving expression to a historical dilemma, the Jansenist tragic hero is seen as unable to accept a valueless world, yet never sure of an alternative since his God is a hidden God. Goldmann detects this structure in a number of Racine's plays; in *Andromaque* the hidden god is Hector, and Andromaque, the tragic heroine, is caught between the demands of an inacceptable world (to which she is tied by the interest of her son) and those of an absent deity. The end of the play is in Goldmann's view a compromise, since Andromaque consents to play a positive part in the life of the 'world'. I do not think that this scheme is necessarily as central to the play as Goldmann suggests, but it does remind us of the importance of religious thinking in the world-view of Racine's contemporaries. Indeed *Andromaque* and most of Racine's other tragedies present us with a flagrant paradox. They appear to express anti-worldly values, but in the form of a dramatic spectacle which was worldly in the extreme and was constantly being attacked by clerics as calculated to inflame the reprehensible passions. And this paradox is perhaps one of the ways in which *Andromaque* reflects most clearly the society of its time—Pyrrhus is both glorious and despicable, just as upper-class worldly values (glory, love, power) are at the same time magnified (by the secular culture) and condemned (by the official religion).

There are doubtless many more relations that could be suggested between Racine's play and contemporary reality. At the most general level one could see the pessimistic side of *Andromaque* as an indirect manifestation of what historians speak of as a century of crisis, a century of bad harvests, plague, internal strife, religious persecution and so on. (If certain nineteenth-century historians saw *le siècle de Louis XIV* as a golden age, its image with modern scholars is much more sombre.) At the time when Racine was writing there was no ideology of progress, no hope of fundamental political or social change. If the world was a bad place, it was also incapable of bettering itself, and could be redeemed only by the intervention of divine providence. And this, it may be said, is what we see in *Andromaque*: people torment and destroy one another, but against all likelihood the hand of providence elevates the humble Andromaque and saves the King of the Trojans. Seventeenth-century audiences were too well indoctrinated to look to secular plays for religious messages, but it seems clear enough from the distance of three hundred years that one part of the structure of the play echoes the Christian myth that was so important for Racine and his contemporaries.

All these historical 'explanations' of *Andromaque* depend on our seeing analogies between one aspect of the play and a corresponding theme in French history. Like most modern works, Racine's tragedy is not the simple expression of one contemporary view, but a sort of sounding-box where many voices converge. The literary, the psychological, and the social are all interwoven. In fact it is the same here as in the previous two chapters: *Andromaque* is an enigmatic object, calling on us to give it a fuller reality. I do not believe we can reach any final or total 'explanation', but by looking outwards from the text to its contemporary surroundings, we shall be enriching our reading and doing some justice to the basic awareness that *Andromaque* is not just there in front of us, but that it was made to meet the needs and desires of Racine and his contemporaries.

All I have said so far concerns the relations between a play and the society that first saw it. It has, however, another and perhaps even more important historical dimension: since 1667 it has been reinterpreted and used by many generations, including our own, and has come to occupy a definite place in the culture and society of France and the other countries where Racine is read or played. This is an immensely complicated story. Through all the variations of interpretation one thing remains clear however: *Andromaque* is and always has been a part of what is variously known as elite culture or high culture. Although it has been published in the French Communist Party series *Les Classiques du Peuple*, it is fair to say that it has never been a genuinely popular classic.

In particular, over the past hundred and fifty years or so, Racine's tragedies have been proposed by the French educational system (and to a certain extent in British schools and universities) as a hallmark of educated taste. Further, the tragic vision of plays such as *Andromaque* has often been set against degenerate modern life and ideas—here, it is implied, is the real thing, far superior to your facile ideas of democracy or progress. It is not surprising if such attitudes generate not only conformist appreciation, but also real antipathy.

But of course all these difficulties exist equally for much of what we call literature; the great books of the past lend themselves alarmingly well to being made instruments of snobbery and mystification. It is up to individual readers or spectators to maintain a critical spirit in deciding what use they should make of the literature which theatres, schools, universities, libraries or books such as the present introduction put before them. I have tried to show not that *Andromaque* embodies in a definitive way any standards of taste or universal truths about humanity, but that it can give us a great deal of pleasure, and a great deal to exercise the mind and imagination. Above all, however, I wish to avoid the stance of the doorman at the Louvre, who is supposed to have said to an unimpressed visitor: 'It is not the pictures that are on trial, Monsieur.' It is all too easy to be eloquent about the classics, so let me finish by emphasizing that my reader may have perfectly good reasons for disliking a play which I personally find both fascinating and moving.